29.9.06

# Women and Bullfighting

# Mediterranea Series

GENERAL EDITOR: Jackie Waldren, *Lecturer at Oxford Brookes University; Research Associate CCCRW, Queen Elizabeth House, Oxford; and Field Co-ordinator, Deya Archaeological Museum and Research Centre, Spain.*

This is a new series which will feature ethnographic monographs and collected works on theoretical approaches to aspects of life and culture in the areas bordering the Mediterranean. Rather than presenting a unified concept of 'the Mediterranean', the aim of the series is to reveal the background and differences in the cultural constructions of social space and its part in patterning social relations among the peoples of this fascinating geographical area.

ISSN: 1354-358X

**Other titles in the series:**

# Women and Bullfighting

## Gender, Sex and the Consumption of Tradition

SARAH PINK

*Oxford • New York*

First published in 1997 by
**Berg**
Editorial offices:
150 Cowley Road, Oxford, OX4 1JJ, UK
70 Washington Square South, New York, NY 10012, USA

Berg is the imprint of Oxford International Publishers Ltd.

**Library of Congress Cataloging-in-Publication Data**

A catalogue record for this book is available from the Library of
Congress.

**British Library Cataloguing-in-Publication Data**

A catalogue record for this book is available from the British
Library.

Front cover photograph: © Sarah Pink

ISBN   1 85973 956 3 (Cloth)
       1 85973 961 X (Paper)

Typeset by JS Typesetting, Wellingborough, Northants.
Printed in the United Kingdom by WBC Bookbinders, Bridgend,
Mid Glamorgan.

# Contents

# Acknowledgements

This book is based on a doctoral thesis presented at the University of Kent, England, in 1995, the research for which was supported by an ESRC award. Since this project began in 1991 I have become indebted to a great many people at each stage of its development: John and Marie Corbin who gave me their support, advice and friendship during my fieldwork and writing up; Richard Sanders, who carried out fieldwork in Córdoba during the same period and with whom I shared ideas and research materials; Ana Martinez for many insights into Spanish anthropology. For their comments at various stages and on different parts of my manuscript I would like to thank John Corbin, John Jervis, Penny Harvey, Neville Colclough and Ursula Sharma. A particular thanks goes to Alan Bicker for his constant support and encouragement.

My research in Córdoba and Andujar led me to meet many people whose contributions were invaluable to my research. It would be impossible to name all of them here. In particular I would like to thank, Encarni Lucena Solís and Eva Pérez Torres for their patience with my Spanish and their friendship; Baldemero Herrero Sánchez de la Puerta, and his family; Rafael Portillo and the staff of the *Museo Taurino*; Manolo Gomez; the *Aula Taurina*; the *Librería M. Sanchez*; Miguel Lozano; *Antoñita La Cordobesa*; Laura and her family.

Finally most thanks of all to Alberto Martinez Rivero who not only made an important contribution to my fieldwork but has lived with me, the thesis and this book ever since.

Acknowledgements

# Prologue: Constructing Femininity and Inventing Tradition

**W**hen I began fieldwork in 1992 few women bullfighters were active in Spain. However, the resources of cultural knowledge that *aficionados* (enthusiasts) drew on to argue their standpoints over whether women ought to bullfight were vast. Locally, in Córdoba (Andalusia), where the majority of my research was based, a young woman who performed as *Antoñita, la Cordobesa* figured in many of these polemics. One summer afternoon the director of the Bullfight Museum, spurred on by my curiosity, determined to seek her out. We agreed that he should arrange for me to meet Antoñita, and he embarked on a series of telephone calls that eventually led him to the house where she was employed as a part-time child minder. Two days later I left my first encounter with Antoñita feeling truly inspired. She appeared pleased and flattered that I had wanted to meet her and learn about women and bullfighting. Whilst we sat outdoors on the patio of a coffee bar in the tourist area of the city Antoñita and I spoke for two hours about her experience of being a bullfighter. She explained why she had loved performing, speaking in terms of a 'special', almost indescribable sensation associated with confronting a bull in the arena. This emotion becomes a reference point in many bullfighters' accounts of the essence of performance. She told me of the people who had helped and supported her, those who had quite unashamedly stood in her way, her motives for giving up her dream to bullfight professionally and how she would cherish the opportunity to continue. The latter, she said could be facilitated only by generous sponsorship. When we parted, our next meeting to visit Miguel who had been Antoñita's trainer and swords handler,

1

had been set for the following week. My meetings with Antoñita continued over a period of two months until she dedicated all her concentration to an intensive programme of training and studying which she hoped would earn her a place in the police force.[1] In Chapter 5 I shall return to her 'story'.

The other woman to whom the discourses of my informants and the media lent a central place was Cristina Sánchez, who in 1996 was Spain's leading woman bullfighter. Cristina's story unfolds in the public eye and in her case I interpret a media narrative rather than a personal self-representation. My interest in these and other women performers was not solely in their own representations of self, but in how they are were represented in a range of local and media discourses.

## Telling Tales and Situating Selves

I was constantly intrigued by informants' subjective interpretations of women bullfighters and especially interested in how the opinions they expressed changed as they resituated themselves in new conversations. Most were unsure of the name of 'our woman bullfighter', or of what had happened to her, and I sensed that their pleasure in citing her existence was combined with an air of indifference to her career. She was related to various different models of gender; a person would convincingly describe Antoñita (or other more famous women performers) as a 'dedicated, good bullfighter' in one breath, to relabel her 'silly and misguided' when someone new entered the conversation. The ways in which people speak of and visualise women bullfighters are often expressions of specific moral ideologies and moral judgements. However, the morality referred to and the ideology being adhered to are dependent upon context. Most often, people's commentaries on the careers and personalities of women bullfighters were built not on a singular image of a woman performer, but on a series of sketches of their own definitions of social reality and order. Thus they represented some of the specific ways in which the notion of a woman bullfighter may be reconciled with particular ways of organising reality. The woman herself was distant from my conversations with informants, as we focused more specifically on what she symbolised for each speaker. For instance, whilst some wove notions of tradition into their constructions of Antoñita's feminine identity, others did not attempt to place her in the categories informed by discourses on tradition.

Antoñita described herself as serious about her commitments, prepared to immerse herself thoroughly in her work and dedicate herself totally to achieving her ambitions. She professed to adore bullfighting and the traditional aspects of Andalusian culture. Comparing her taste to that of her friends who enjoyed discos and loud pop music, she stated her preference for the Spanish *copla* or flamenco. Antoñita said she believed that in general women can do anything that men can. Personally speaking, she needed an outdoor job with variety, that involved something she cared about, she could not face the idea of repetitive office work. Our conversations did not feel trivial; I gained the impression that Antoñita cared deeply for bullfighting, but had been unable to dedicate another five years to it in the awareness that she would, in all likelihood, finish no closer to her dream. She attributed her failure partly to the lack of training facilities and financial backing available in Córdoba. Rather than bragging about her own abilities or potential as a bullfighter, Antoñita lamented that she had been unable to acquire sufficient experience or improve her technique. She modestly suggested that she had been 'one of the worst' women bullfighters.

Whilst Antoñita's self-representation does not correlate directly with binary gender models of traditional bullfighting discourse, informants often described her in the terms of such discourse. Different people used these local reference points to classify Antoñita in contradictory ways. I did not recognise Antoñita from the description which was given me by one informant before I met her. I suspected that my informant's description of her appearance was an elaboration upon a vague memory. Antoñita later told me they had met only once, at a media event two years earlier. This man described Antoñita as pretty, dark haired, tall, slim, and shy: a typical *Cordobesa*. His visualisation of her represented the traditional Cordoban feminine beauty associated with the work of the early twentieth-century artist Julio Romero de Torres. He was referring to a (once hegemonic) local discourse on feminine beauty and morality and gender role segregation. Moreover, by introducing Antoñita in this courteous style he was simultaneously performing a self-representation of traditional masculinity and integrity.

The woman who stood in the opposite corner of the plaza wearing a green suit and holding a motorcycle helmet under her arm was to my eyes evidently not the stereotype of local beauty described by my informant. She did not comply with the generalised image of womanhood represented in traditionalist discourse on gender.

Furthermore, neither Antoñita's self-representation nor my impressions of her fitted the category which was set up by another informant who had wished to express his disapproval of her activities. He had described Antoñita as a bad bullfighter, and not a true *aficionada*. Instead, he claimed that she had 'just wanted everyone to look at her' and to 'say how good she looked'. In constructing this representation of Antoñita he was referring to a local traditional model of a (male) bullfighter. Other informants told me that certain modes of behaviour are expected of bullfighters but are simply not appropriate for a woman – 'bullfighters spit, shout, frequent bars and womanise'. My informant juxtaposed his negative evaluation of Antoñita with a description of a 'true *aficionada*'. In his opinion, this woman 'would have been a bullfighter if she was a man', but as a woman she had stayed in her proper place as a committed and informed spectator. Representations of gender ambiguity were integral to these informants' delineations of the woman bullfighter. The categories they used to associate particular meanings and values with her and to either approve or critique her were not fixed: when it was convenient to their perspectives she was reframed by other reference points and evaluated in a different light. In addition they contrast with Antoñita's self-representations. These subjectivities constructed the personality and behaviour of Antoñita in strikingly different ways.[2] One branded her a misfit by characterising her behaviour as wrong and ridiculous, the other treated her as a normal girl with a silly dream.

Curiously the three narratives, including Antoñita's own, used the notion of 'tradition' as a point of reference.[3] Each commentator defined tradition and simultaneously situated both their own self and women bullfighters in a particular (and different) relation to it. Antoñita saw her bullfighting as traditional and comparable with other metaphors for tradition – flamenco and *coplas* – all opposed to discos and night-clubs. For her, the enacting of tradition did not entail conforming to rules of gender segregation. In contrast, the description of Antoñita as an embodiment of traditional feminine morality identified her precisely with a gender segregation model. This point of view rather than representing Antoñita as a bullfighter, constructed her femininity in opposition to the bullfighter's masculinity. In the third example Antoñita is criticised precisely for not expressing traditional femininity and she is stripped of all the virtue that according to the former informant she embodied. Many other informants, however, did not find female sex irreconcilable with a bullfighting identity. A theory of the plurality of gender permits an understanding of how people with very different perspectives on both gender and bullfighting were able to argue that there was no reason why Antoñita should not successfully bullfight. Many labelled any opposition to her as 'sexist', and no doubt they pledged their support to her for a whole range of particular motives.

## Consuming Contemporary Tradition

Antoñita gave up her quest to become a bullfighter in the early 1990s, but during this period several other young women performers were achieving a moderate amount of success. Women bullfighters are situated by a range of different discourses and subjectivities on gender, bullfighting and tradition in a diverse 1990s consumer society. In particular, women's bullfighting raises questions concerning local definitions of tradition. For instance, what should be the boundaries of behaviour which adheres to traditional morality and what measures should be taken to preserve the integrity of tradition? These questions are neither simply nor uniformly answered. In some contexts women bullfighters are able to appeal to tradition insofar as they are participating in a traditional activity and conforming to the rules set by established tradition (Hobsbawm 1983: 2),[4] except of course they defy one vital norm – that of the gender of the performer. In this situation the tradition as structured procedure is untouched. Conversely if that tradition is redefined as a living event that does not exist without its participants, then its established composition is challenged by the introduction of women performers. Women bullfighters break 'the rules which permit or constrain . . . participation' (Lewis 1980: 12) but still insist that they are taking part in the bullfight 'properly'. Lewis emphasises that such customs are justified by tradition, in the sense that 'our ancestors have always done things this way' (ibid). The argument for the exclusion of women performers is sometimes justified by an appeal to tradition, but this is not always accepted as a good enough reason for the practice of an exclusionist policy which clashes with the values of many people. The subjectivity of the aficionado is crucial to the specific meanings which he/she invests in different gendered performers. In the following chapters I show how for some informants women's participation was non-problematic, whilst others were afraid that it threatened the integrity of the event.

Contemporary local perspectives on the traditional bullfight and other rituals may be understood in relation to other social and cultural aspects of contemporary Andalusia. In Chapter 1 these connections are explored with reference to discourses relating to sexuality and work. The gender roles played out in traditional ritual performances and events are frequently at variance with the morality and aspirations of their participants (see Pink 1997b). Many aficionados disagree with the traditional gender roles which they see as epitomised by the male performer. Nevertheless, they are able to appreciate the professional bullfight regardless of the sex of the performer, a fact which is congruent with Lewis's point that the very indeterminacy of ritual lends it significance and 'contains a way of seeing that ritual may survive, still seem worth doing, offering some feeling of continuity, message and enrichment' for people throughout periods of social change (1980: 38). However, a woman's performance – if it is to be considered the same ritual – begs further questions about the relationship between ritual and society. Some people are demanding that the public 'ruling'(ibid. 19) of this ritual should correspond to non-traditional gender configurations. Tradition fails to justify consistently the 'ruling' against women performers. In Chapter 2, I shall critique existing anthropological treatments of the bullfight as ritual, to suggest how women performers may be appropriately incorporated into its analysis.

The bullfight is in an ambiguous situation: it is a traditional ritual in a changing and diverse social and cultural context.[5] Contemporary gender relations are discussed in Chapter 1, whilst the success of women in bullfighting as performers, critics, journalists, photographers, managers and aficionadas is detailed in Chapters 4 to 8. In Chapter 3 some of the tensions between the roles set out for women in the traditional discourse of bullfighting and women's actual experience are discussed. In the 1990s, bullfighting culture is obliged to accommodate non-traditional gender models in a way which correlates with the changing attitudes towards work and sexuality in Andalusia outlined in Chapter 1 (see also Pink 1997c). Furthermore, the bullfight is a living tradition and a commercial enterprise which must be both contemporary and traditional in order to satisfy the broad range of its potential audience. Media producers and the live performance contract-makers are therefore obliged to develop the bullfight as a marketable tradition,[6] a practice that inevitably involves the commodification of both performers and performance. Therefore, I explore the role of women performers in what may be called 'contemporary–traditional' bullfighting. Finally, in Chapter 8, taking the media bullfight as central to this contemporary–traditional bullfight culture, I discuss how women performers are incorporated into late twentieth-century bullfighting culture.

## Notes

1. On reflection these conversations possibly rekindled Antoñita's interest in bullfighting, summoning memories of the ambition she once had. When I first met her she saw little of Miguel and his family, and appeared to have broken some of her links with bullfighting. My investigation may have reintensified these connections.

2. Whilst it is possible that Antoñita represented herself to each informant differently, the example still indicates their strategies for expressing critique and their own self-representation.

3. My informants used the terms 'tradition' and 'traditional' to speak of activities, relationships and objects that satisfied their own particular definitions of these concepts. I qualify my own use of these terms by recognising that their meanings are not fixed. Neither the bullfight nor particular gender relations are essentially 'traditional'.

4. In his definition of tradition, Hobsbawm (1983: 2) distinguishes between the rigid and repeated character of traditional activities and the greater flexibility of 'custom'.

5. See also Pérez Molina (1991) who notes the lack of cohesion between the bullfight and contemporary urban culture.

6. The 1990s have seen, in broadcasting throughout Europe, a demise in public-service broadcasting institutions, and a general tendency away 'from service to business' (Ang 1991: 104).

# Introduction: A World of Bullfighting

T he central theme of this book is an interpretation of the recent success of women bullfighters in Spain[1]. In the following chapters the visible popularity of women performers and the other diverse roles that women play in bullfighting are situated in a contemporary consumer society where 'traditional' and 'modern' lifestyles are continuously created, performed and redefined. The construction, consumption and appropriation of media narratives and technology are intricately woven into contemporary understandings and experiences of the bullfight. Thus the live performance will be considered in terms of this media domain of cultural production. Gendered identities are understood as plural, negotiated and partial; they are completed only in the act of definition. My main thesis will be that an analysis of how subjectivities and representations of self and others are related to a range of discourses on gender and bullfighting is fundamental to an understanding of why and how women bullfighters may succeed in the 1990s. The ethnography describes the experiences of women in the 'bullfighting world', the discourses that approve and disapprove of their activity, and how these may be related to a wider Andalusian culture. Thus I propose a reworking of existing analyses of gender and the bullfight in Andalusia.

## Arrival in Andalusia . . . and the State of Spain

This book is based on fieldwork in, and a continuing association with, Andalusia between 1992 and 1996. Andalusia is not exactly uncharted territory in anthropology. Andalusian villages have often provided material for the 'community study' tradition in the British and North American anthropology of Pitt-Rivers (1963), Gilmore (for example, 1987a, 1995) and Brandes (for example, 1981). The

Andalusian city has featured in particular in Press's work on Seville (1979) and Corbin and Corbin's research in Ronda (1984, 1986). Some recent work of the 1990s has taken a more thematic approach by considering aspects of Andalusian culture. For example, Crain (1992) focused on the *Rocío* pilgrimage, whilst Washabaugh (1996) analyses flamenco. Spanish anthropologists have also paid significant attention to Andalusia; for example, Rodríguez Becerra (1984) and Serran Pagan's (1980) critique of Pitt-River's ethnography of Grazelema.

Pitt-Rivers, Gilmore and Brandes are the authors of some of the more problematic works which I shall discuss in Chapter 1 and Mitchell (1991) has also attempted to inscribe an ethnocentric definition of 'the Spanish' into what is now a more resistant landscape. Spanish academic protest has allowed the 'other' to be heard (for example, Catédra (ed.) 1991), but the orientalisation of Andalusia continues in the hands of Mitchell (1991, 1994) and Pitt-Rivers (1996) (cf. MacClancey 1996; Washabaugh 1996). This notion of Spain as a modern, western 'other within' has been widespread. The journalist Hooper suggested that the 1992 Seville EXPO would 'propel one of the poorest areas of one of the poorest countries in western Europe out of the pre-industrial and into the post-industrial world' (1992). Some Spaniards, romantic foreigners and anthropologists claim that Spain and the Spanish possess an uncivilised, irrational element which is often idealised as a lost piece of our Northern European past. The bullfight, flamenco and a code of 'honour and shame' are amongst the aspects of Spanish culture usually attributed to this passionate, irrational aspect supposedly obliterated by the rationalising force of the Enlightenment in the rest of Europe (Douglass 1992). Spain is thus located by some as of 'the west' but pertaining to 'the rest of the west'. These very problematic assumptions have been directed in particular at Andalusia. Their bearing on anthropological constructions of gender and the bullfight are discussed in Chapter 1.

Initially I carried out my fieldwork in Andalusia from 1992 to 1994. For most of this time I was based, and lived, in the city of Córdoba, the capital of the province of the same name. This was complemented by a short period in Seville, and four months spent in village and rural settings of the Sierra Morena, a mountain range in Jaén province, northern Andalusia. From 1994 to 1996 I have maintained contact though frequent visits, telephone calls, e-mail and letters, and the continued analysis of media materials. The city of Córdoba has a population of over 200,000, and is in a hot dry zone where temperatures can reach over 45 °C during the summer.[2] Situated in the centre of Andalusia, Córdoba is 140 kilometres north of Seville along the motorway which leads to Madrid and the north of Spain, and is easily accessible by road and rail. To the immediate north of the city is a mountainous Sierra and to the south are large dry plains. Many Cordobans are well versed in a version of local history which is dominated by the Moorish influence of the Arabic rulers who were in power for several centuries. The historic area in the centre of the old quarter of the city attracts international tourists who are attracted by its ancient *Mezquita* and *Patios*.

## A World of Bullfighting

Local bullfight aficionados claim that Córdoba is the centre of the bullfighting world. Although there is a long and impressive history of bullfighting in the city, the same claim has been made for many other cities by their inhabitants, and the Cordoban version reflects what some informants critically referred to as Cordoban 'provincialism'. Nevertheless, the city's aficionados are extremely proud of the prominent place that Córdoba and some of its local heroes occupy in the 'history of bullfighting'. There is an extensive literature on bullfighting in Córdoba which is supported by an active local community of bullfighting journalists, critics and photographers. Most social bullfighting activity takes place in the city's thriving network of bullfighting clubs. Generally referred to as the *peñas*, these groups are most active during the winter when the bullfighting season is over. The municipal bullfighting museum houses a large collection of historic bullfighting paraphernalia, and a library where I spent many hours in study and in discussion. The city has a large modern bullring, built in the 1970s, where performances regularly take place during the spring and autumn, and in which a bullfighting school is held during the winter months. Several practising and retired bullfighters live in and near the city, their lives, successes and failures are part of daily news and everyday conversation within bullfighting circles. They are amongst the local bullfighting celebrities and usually play active roles in the social and formal events of the bullfighting world. This research location offered me an environment in which bullfighting is learnt, performed, discussed, debated, recorded and photographed. Both the producers and interpreters of the event were readily available; and I was able to observe and participate in the processes by which

**Figure 1:** This photograph of Cristina Sánchez, her father (left) and her Cordoban hosts (right) features the group in a frequently photographed tourist site. This composition includes the tower of the *Mezquita*, an important icon in local history and tourism and follows a similar format to postcards of the location.
© Sarah Pink

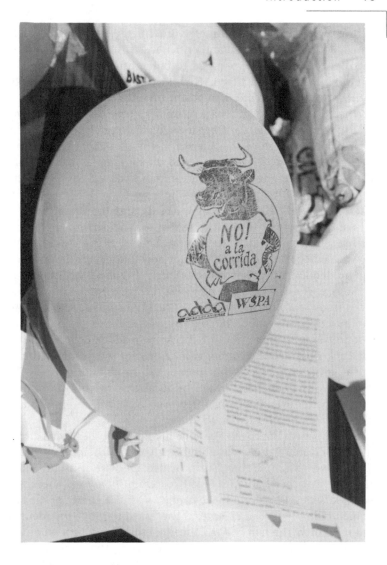

**Figure 2:** The anti-bullfighting campaign and its material culture are part of the contemporary context in which the bullfight is understood. This iconography formed the mainstay of an ADDA campaign in Madrid in 1992. In Córdoba I met many people who were fervently opposed to the bullfight but in my experience there was no public confrontation or campaign in the city.

© Sarah Pink

information about the bullfight is interpreted, represented, published, collected, exhibited and criticised. Yet many of my informants were indifferent or opposed to bullfighting, some thought it immoral. I discovered that it is also possible to live in Córdoba without bullfighting culture imposing on one's life.

When I arrived in Córdoba I spoke very little Spanish. As I was able to read the language I began archival research in the library located in the office of the director of the municipal bullfighting museum, the *Museo Taurino*. I entered the museum as an academic, a student researching for a thesis, and also became involved with the University's *Aula Taurina* (bullfighting forum). My academic interest was taken seriously by students and the director alike. Whilst they thought it remarkable that an English woman should pursue such a course of investigation the idea that a thesis should be written about *tauromaquia* was not novel; intellectual discussion and academic writing about the bullfight is considered normal in Andalusia. The first people I met were most accommodating: I was given study space in the museum office, invitations to social events and introductions to local bullfighting personalities. From my daily base in the museum, I not only began to read about bullfighting, but I also observed the comings and goings of the people involved in the local production and representation of bullfighting. The museum was frequently visited by local writers and journalists, several special events are organised every year and receptions and speeches are often hosted on its *patio*.

As my Spanish improved I became involved in other social circles and participated in several bullfighting clubs. Although my initial contact with the museum had provided me with a useful social identity, in other contexts I had to establish myself anew. For example, when I began to make contact with the family of the late woman bullfighter Maria Gomez, I was asked to prove my identity and reliability. The family was concerned that I may be a journalist and by speaking with me they may be risking the publication of potentially damaging information. It was my status as an academic that convinced them of my trustworthiness.

There were many situations which I considered would be inappropriate for me to enter as a single woman. This problem was usually resolved by the company of men or women friends. Whilst I was able to develop strategies for participating in situations not normally either open, or of interest, to women, my gender did not allow me to be involved in many others. My Andalusian partner carried out much of the research into male discourse which I would never have had access to as a woman. Writers who emphasise the comparative ease with which women are able to enter 'male worlds', whereas men tend to be excluded from women's domains have constructed an unjustified binary distinction (see Delamont 1995: 180–1).

## A Photographic Field

In order to combat my linguistic limitations and the problematic 'single woman alone' status I often took on a role of photographer. At the start of my fieldwork my camera became an armour, a learning device and a means of expanding and reinforcing my social network. As an armour it rescued me from 'standing around', looking, but able to say very little to those to whom I was introduced. When I was busy taking photos I was occupied and able to document social occasions. The photographs were appreciated by the event's organisers and participants, and this helped me to forge new relationships. I became involved in networks through which images were exchanged, I participated in the creation of visual 'memories' for my informants and was able to witness how people selected their images, that is, how they constructed their visual histories. The requests I received for photographs to pass on to others revealed social relations and networking strategies. I adopted similar strategies myself in my research and personal life.[3] Significantly, I participated in the production of the visual culture of bullfighting: a crucial element of the world of bullfighting.

I began fieldwork as a foreign student barely speaking Spanish and left an 'expert' on women bullfighters. I won a journalistic photography prize for a photograph of Cristina Sánchez (see Pink 1996b, 1997a). I was interviewed by a local journalist who published an article about myself and my work; took part in a live radio programme to speak about women bullfighters and photography; and my own articles about women and bullfighting were published in a local bullfighting journal and newspaper (Pink 1993a,b,c, 1994). I spent many lunchtimes and evenings watching the same television programmes as millions of Spanish people, and I came to organise my own life around a routine very similar to those of my informants. My experiences of being a woman in Andalusia and in the world of bullfighting form an integral part of this project, as do the media narratives and visual communications with which I became involved.

**Figure 3:** This reproduction of an early C20 (circa 1910) studio portrait of the bullfighter *Machaquito* was given to me during my first weeks of fieldwork. Both historical and contemporary photography are actively produced and circulated in bullfighting circles. These images form part of the material culture of the bullfighting world and are woven into its discourses and debates.

## The Contemporary Bullfight

In the 1990s the Spanish bullfight[4] is a controversial event amongst both Spaniards and foreigners. Yet for a large number of people, commonly referred to as aficionados, bullfighting is a central element of their leisure time. During the most intense part of the Spanish bullfighting season, which runs from spring to autumn, bullfights are held almost every day in one of Spain's bullrings. At the height of the summer season weekend bullfights are held concurrently in many cities, towns and villages. Indeed this activity is not restricted to Spain and the bullfight is also popular in southern France, Portugal,[5] Mexico, Peru and other Latin American countries. Performances are well attended by an audience of men, women and children of all ages. The more important bullfights are televised and most are photographed. Bullfighting is big business, and whilst most aficionados do not consider it a primarily commercial enterprise, it generates much capital and employment, not only within the bullfighting world itself, but in communication and media and all the industries which serve it. Despite Spanish and international campaigns against it,[6] the bullfight is not dying out and at the time of writing it seems unlikely that the European Parliament will succeed in prohibiting it (cf. Pitt-Rivers 1993). Bullfighting is popular amongst aficionados of all ages, and many young people also actively participate in its production and performance.

The iconography of the bullfight is centred on the *torero* figure: the individual triumphant masculine hero (cf. Pink 1997a). Yet despite the gender stereotypes represented in bullfighting culture and in the traditionalism of its dominant discourse, women are becoming increasingly active in the bullfighting world.

## The Standard Performance

Most performances take place in the late afternoon and last for approximately two hours. In a standard bullfight three bullfighters kill six bulls, each performer having been allocated two in the *sorteo* which takes place in the morning. The sorteo entails a kind of lottery in which the numbers of the three pairs of bulls (the pairs are selected so the best bull is likely to be matched with the worst) are written on folded pieces of paper drawn by the performers or their representatives. Bullfighters perform in order of seniority – he/she who is most advanced in his/her career takes the first and fourth bulls.[7]

**Figure 4:** The performers moving their capes in the ring before retiring to the ringside for the start of the performance.
© Sarah Pink

**Figure 5:** Cristina Sánchez performing with the cape
© Sarah Pink

**Figure 6:** Cristina Sánchez performing with the *muleta*
© Sarah Pink

**Figure 7:** A male bullfighter performing with the *muleta*
© Sarah Pink

The beginning of the performance is marked by the entry of the *alguaciles*, mounted officials who ride into the arena ahead of the three bullfighters, followed by their respective *cuadrillas* of three *banderilleros* and two *picadores*. The cuadrilla is the *matador's* team of three banderilleros and two picadores, whom he pays to perform with him. The banderillero places the *banderillas* (barbed sticks) in to the neck muscle of the bull. A banderillero is usually a bullfighter who failed to make the grade as a matador. This is, however, still a dangerous role, and although it is an infrequent occurrence, one banderillero was killed in the bullring during my fieldwork. The role of the picador is to damage the neck muscles of the bull by spiking it with a lance. The picador is mounted on a sturdy horse which is blindfolded. His own and the horse's bodies are well padded to protect them from injury. The picador in general is characterised as an unpopular figure (normally owing to the damage which he does to the bull). He tends to be the least respected member of the cuadrilla and the most frequently ridiculed by the audience. The *matador de toros* is literally the 'killer of bulls'. Whilst all performers may be referred to as toreros, it is only the matador de toros who performs with, and actually kills, fully grown four–year–old bulls in public.

Once they have entered and crossed the bullring, the performers salute the *presidente*[8] who governs the performance and then they retire to their respective positions at the ringside. On the release of the first bull the bullfight begins. During the twenty minutes allowed for each animal the following procedure is played out:

The matador's assistants attract the bull with their capes to 'test' it whilst the matador and his advisors contemplate its characteristics. The matador himself then steps out to perform a series of cape passes until the presidente calls for the introduction of the picadores. With the assistance of the matador and banderilleros the picador tempts the bull to charge him so that he may lance its neck. This is repeated two or three times before the picadores leave the ring and the stage of the banderilleros begins. Sometimes the matador performs this role himself but more usually two banderilleros alternate. Taking one banderilla in each hand the banderillero attracts the bull with the movement of his body by running towards the animal, leaping to one side to insert the banderillas. Once the six banderillas are in place the final stage of the performance begins: the matador exchanges his pink cape for the red muleta and sword and now steps out to perform alone with the bull. After what is ideally a successful series of muleta passes, the matador changes swords and kills the bull. If he/she performs well the audience will ask that trophies of the bull's ears (and for an outstanding performance, the tail) be awarded to the triumphant performer. Even if no trophies are granted, a successful performance merits a victory lap during which the matador is thrown gifts, hats, flowers and other objects by the audience. The dead bull is dragged out of the arena by a team of mules and the sanded surface is smoothed for the next performer.

Bullfighting is dangerous. Not all performers are successful, and whilst bullfighters are rarely killed they are frequently injured. The informants I spoke with judged that on average one bullfighter is killed every year.

## The Career of a Bullfighter

The performance described above would be enacted by a professional bullfighter. Most performances follow the same format, although at the initial stages of a performer's career when he/she fights smaller bulls, the picador stage is excluded. The young performer passes from being a *becerrista* (fighting one-year-old animals) to a *novillero sin picadores* (who fights two to three-year-old bulls[9] without picadores), to a novillero with picadores who is differentiated from the torero by the age and weight of the bulls he/she fights. The début with picadores is a significant step towards the final stage of promotion through the *alternativa*. Thus the performer graduates to full torero status and fights four-year-old bulls at professional level. Whilst many aspire to be bullfighters and reach the first stages, it is very difficult to succeed as a fully fledged professional.

As I write in 1996, no woman bullfighter has taken the alternativa in Spain. However in May 1996 Cristina Sánchez did so in Nîmes in France which is on the Spanish circuit, and thus she holds torero status. At the close of the 1993 season, during my fieldwork, six women bullfighters were active at the novillero level and Cristina Sánchez maintained a position amongst the top ten male novilleros with picadores throughout most of the season. Of the others, Mari Paz Vega, Yolanda Carvajal and Laura Valencia performed with picadores and Mireílle Ayura and Soría Diáz sin picadores. They received favourable reviews and media attention, contracts for live performances (sometimes televised) and trophies. In 1993, whilst Cristina Sánchez performed in 34 *corridas* (bullfights) and collected 51 ears, the top male torero Enrique Ponce performed an exceptional 110 times and cut 135 ears (*Aplausos* 18 October 1993). Status is measured in terms of the number of performances and trophies awarded and listings are regularly published. In the same year, five women *rejoneadoras* (horseback bullfighters) were also active. The successful Maria Sara was extremely popular and classified amongst the top rejoneadores. In 1996 the picture was changing as Cristina Sánchez took centre stage on the professional scene.

During my fieldwork in Córdoba four women became the main reference points in discussions of women bullfighters: Conchita Cintrón, a rejoneadora active in the 1950s; Antoñita (see above); Maria Gomez, a local woman who had performed in the 1930s; and Cristina Sánchez who, as she became increasingly famous, became the focus of informants commentaries between 1993 and 1996. Whilst all of these women feature in the discussions of the following chapters, Cristina Sánchez plays a central role in this book. The focus on this particular woman performer was inevitable simply owing to the extent to which she was privileged in aficionado, media and other discourses on women bullfighters. This book explores a set of contexts for which she became a significant icon.

# Notes

1. In previous papers (for example, Pink 1996a) I have, in common with other writers (for example, Marvin 1988; MacClancey 1996), written of female bullfighters. This terminology sits uncomfortably with the plurality of gender I want to discuss, thus in this book I refer to women bullfighters, assuming 'women' to be a heterogeneous category.

2. During July, August and September the city grinds to a halt. Many shops close down for the summer months and most businesses close for at least one month. Those Cordobans who have family or second homes at the beach or in the mountains, or who can afford to rent an apartment elsewhere, leave the city until the cooler temperatures arrive at the end of September. The only people to be seen on the streets of Córdoba on a hot summer lunchtime are foreign tourists. The locals surface at night, but social life tends to be concentrated in the cooler outskirts which rise into the Sierra north of the city rather than in the centre. Similarly, the activities of the bullfighting world in Córdoba are curtailed during the summer; it is too hot for performances and social life is located elsewhere.

3. This type of photographic activity provokes the question of the role of the anthropologist in creating his/her own data, in this case, my own

images. Whilst I framed my shots, I always did so in terms of the knowledge that I had accumulated about my subjects' preferred style of photography: I tried to conform to an established journalistic style. There is nothing wrong with anthropologists creating their own images, or visual texts, however, it is important to be aware of how, why and for whom these images were created. Elsewhere (Pink 1997g) I explore the photographic research process in detail in a multimedia text.

4. The notion of the 'Spanish Bullfight' is expressed amongst aficionados. I qualify my use of the term by noting that the concept of 'Spanishness' is problematic. There are regional variations in the Spanish bullfight as regards the time of the event, clothing of officials, and additional elements of the performance. However, these do not affect the structure of the performance which is governed by a uniform set of rules.

5. The Portuguese bullfight has some variations from the Spanish version. The most frequently cited (especially amongst anti-bullfight campaigners) is that the bull is not killed in public.

6. The Spanish campaigns are mainly based north of Andalusia. Although I heard of a fairly large group in Cádiz, in Córdoba I witnessed no public anti-bullfighting activity. Although many of my informants were against bullfighting – mainly on grounds of cruelty to animals – in general, rather than active opposition, I encountered indifference.

7. Not all bullfights follow this standard model. Some are 'mixed' in which both rejoneadores and toreros or novilleros perform.

8. The presidente (who is also the representative of the law) is empowered with controlling the bullfight: he may overrule the decisions of the performers and he decides whether to award trophies.

9. Such young and small bulls are not considered to be sufficiently strong or dangerous enough to be subjected to the lances of the picadores.

# Part 1

# Rethinking Gender and Bullfighting in Andalusia

In Chapters 1 and 2 I critically evaluate existing literature relating to gender and bullfighting in Andalusia. The theories proposed by these two overlapping bodies of literature fail to accommodate women bullfighters, whilst the ethnography describes an Andalusian culture that renders women performers inappropriate in the arena of professional bullfighting. I propose that the contemporary success of women bullfighters as well as the inconsistencies between my own research findings and the existing ethnography, demand a reassessment of gender relations in Andalusia and a rethinking of how anthropology may theorise both gender and the bullfight in Andalusia.

# Slaying Anthropology's Goat: Men, Women and Reputation in Andalusia

## Ethnographies of Andalusia and Anthropological Constructions of Gender

Most existing analyses of gender in Andalusia originate from the 1980s and take on board an emphasis on the cultural construction of gender characteristic of that period. Inherent to this theory of gender is an insistence that an empirically evidenced cross-cultural gender hierarchy perpetuated the universal subordination of women (see Ortner and Whitehead 1981). This approach has been criticised in the 1990s and in particular its essentialist treatment of the relationship between sex and gender has been questioned. Instead an approach that also accounts for how 'cultures actually construct sex differences between men and women' (Moore 1993b: 196) is advocated.[1] A related movement to acknowledge the importance of the biology and the 'embodied' character of gender, identity and experience has similarly problematised the social constructivist approach to gender.[2] An emphasis on the plurality of gender models which replaces a binary gender system, stresses differences amongst, rather than solely between, men and women. This perspective, combined with a notion of gendered identities as subjective and negotiated, questions the fixity of both identity and gender. Such a concept of identity can be extended in order to regard the gendered self as completed and defined only in relation to other selves, subjectivities, discourses, representations or material objects (see, for example, Kulick 1995: 17–18[3]). Other work on identity and self-hood (for example, Cohen 1994) focuses on the 'self-driven' and 'pro-active' self to explore the relationship between (amongst other things) knowledge and experience and culture. In this chapter I critique the existing literature on gender in Andalusia to develop a perspective on Andalusian gender-relations which accounts for diversity, subjectivity, the body and experience.

The ethnographic accounts of Pitt-Rivers (1963), Gilmore (1985) and Brandes (1981) in particular, have worked with a binary, essentialist and hierarchical definition of gender-relations. This literature fixes gender, identity and experience within rigid categories. These frameworks and assumptions have formed the basis for the anthropological models of 'honour and shame' which I will argue are utterly inappropriate for understanding how prestige and reputation are associated with particular gendered identities and specific men and women in contemporary Andalusia. A 'patriarchy' model (advanced by, for example, Borrell 1992; Cousins 1994) is similarly inadequate for understanding the complexities and contradictions of gender in contemporary Andalusia. I propose to locate my discussion of discourses on women bullfighters in a less evenly textured social and cultural scene

## Oppressed in Anthropological Texts and Imprisoned by Theory

Corbin and Corbin's ethnography of the Andalusian city of Ronda indicates how gender role segregation is not essentially related to women's oppression (see 1986: 69–70). Corbin and Corbin's argument develops in part as a response to Gilmore's agreement with Ortner and Whitehead (1981: 6) that 'this hierarchical gender structure [is] a basic "organising" principle in andro-centric societies like those of Southern Europe' (Gilmore 1985: 2). Corbin and Corbin's case that, in the 1970s, gender role segregation was instrumental in restricting competition between men and women is convincing. Yet their interpretation appears to have been smothered by the dominant anthropological model of hierarchical gender-relations represented in the work of Ortner and Whitehead. Other ethnographers who reported the experience of gender in terms of hierarchy and oppression used frameworks which allowed their work to support Ortner and Whitehead's model. In particular, Brandes's and Pitt-Rivers's work was taken seriously as empirical evidence by Ortner and Whitehead who criticised Pitt-Rivers for under-emphasising the importance of prestige (1981: 13). Thus defining 'a gender system' as 'first and foremost a prestige structure itself' (ibid.: 16), Ortner and Whitehead treated the '"Honour" and "shame" complex of the Mediterranean' as an important example (ibid.: 15) of how cross-culturally 'cross-sex social relations in all their manifestations . . . ramify upon male prestige from the point of view of the male actor' (ibid.: 18). This interpretation constructs a linear one-way movement of prestige from women, to domains shared by men and women and finally to men: it leaves no space for women's prestige and it accounts for only one category of masculine prestige.

Ortner and Whitehead call on ethnography to justify their perspective by noting that a 'tendency to define women relationally' was exhibited by informants. I suggest that the gaze be redirected towards the tendencies of anthropologists. I would like to pose two questions. First, who defines women relationally? and second, what are the different contexts and criteria for the evaluation of an individual's prestige and reputation? In Andalusia, male anthropologists have defined women's worlds and inter-sex domains as subordinate and supportive to masculine spheres. The masculine bias written into both ethnography and theory of gender in the so-called Mediterranean (cf. Lindisfarne 1994) has been noted particularly in the work of Brandes. His research, interpretation and representation of Andalusian culture developed from a masculine standpoint that led to his construction of an 'unbalanced' representation of gender relations (cf. Loizos 1992)[4] that renders women subordinate to men. Yet women researchers have shown that masculine prestige systems are not necessarily the only organising principle of 'Mediterranean societies' (see Hart 1994; Lindisfarne 1994).

In the 1990s I participated in situations where gender role segregation and gender hierarchies are represented in a variety of different ways in public discourse and through the performance of daily life. Simultaneously, other competitive and co-operative relations between and amongst different men and women were equally prevalent. Gender segregation and hierarchies are contested models in contemporary Spain. Some Andalusians deny having experienced them, others cite them as the source for their frustration. The discourses are open, public, political, and diverse; they are represented by the media and by politicians in different ways. For example, campaigns initiated by the Andalusian branch of the governmental *Instituto de la Mujer*, the department that promotes sexual equality and women's issues, ran a series of television advertisements depicting a cartoon version of a model family – two parent and two child. Both parents work, and all family members share domestic work and enjoy their weekend leisure together (in together (in this instance, family bike-rides in the park). In contrast, in Córdoba during the 1994 regional election campaigns, the final words of the speech made by a candidate for the Andalusian Party called on his audience to vote for the good of 'your future, your wives, your children and your jobs'. I found that both these discourses are referred to, manipulated, critiqued and made meaningful in a range of different ways in everyday conversation.[5]

In common with Gilmore, some Spanish feminist ethnographers have followed Ortner and Whitehead (1981) to argue that women's oppression is a structural reality and must be combatted. For instance, Borrell (1992) argues that women are trapped within a male-dominated society (see Pink 1997c). Less extreme than Gilmore, for whom women tend to be the domestic pawns in men's public games (1985: 5), is the standpoint of Sanchíz et al. (1992) which represents a quest to liberate Andalusian housewives from domestic imprisonment and misery, and to educate women in general. This entails a commitment to promoting change both within the family and in the public sphere, it shares a point of view similar to that of the television sequence described above. Community based self-help and self-awareness groups through which women are encouraged to realise their own self-worth have been set up. They engage in projects such as the rewriting of women's history, the boosting of women's self-confidence, and the introduction of fulfilling areas of social and cultural activity; and they are reported to produce very positive results. Nevertheless, the success of practical policies that are based on theories of women's subordination does not justify the argument that a domination/subordination model mirrors all women's experience. Significantly, such an argument does not allow for the plurality of experiences of gender proposed by the theory and ethnography of the 1990s.[6] Whilst rigid models of gender role segregation and women's subordination may sometimes appear to be convincing explanations for the situations in which particular women find themselves, it does not follow that they form an overarching organisational structure in 'the culture at large'. In the 1990s, hierarchy and subordination are sometimes incorporated into Andalusian women's representations of their own experiences. In particular, when women and men compete for the same jobs a recognition of 'male dominance' may often seem the most relevant interpretation of a woman's experience. For instance, in the case of Antoñita, the Cordoban woman bullfighter, her inability to gain equal access to resources in the bullfighting world was coupled with some men's attempts to restrict her progress and obstruct her ambition. Her situation may have been experienced, and could be understood, as a woman being constantly pushed back by a wall of masculine dominance. This analysis, however, would not serve as a definitive or systemic explanation for her failure to succeed in bullfighting. In contrast, I would argue that she was judged in a range of rather different ways by a variety of subjectivities. In what follows I shall focus briefly on sexuality and work to illustrate the fluidity of gender-relations. I shall identify some circumstances in which gender hierarchies and subordination may be perceived and experienced and others in which they are not. Whilst some men may appear more powerful than some women in one social context, it does not follow that all women are always inferior to all men. Hierarchies may be rapidly reversed or reordered amongst the same group of people as they are resituated in a new set of negotiations. Moreover, in bullfighting some women are the holders of power and the gatekeepers to certain resources. If 'gender hierarchy' is to be maintained as a useful concept in anthropology it is surely more instrumentally defined as one which is contextual and subject to reorganisation, rather than an idea which is static and based solely on sexual difference.

## The End of Honour?: copulation, gender and reputation

So-called Mediterranean concepts of honour and shame have dominated the study of gender in Andalusia during the last forty years since the 1950s. Despite Lever's (1986) insightful suggestion that honour may be a 'red herring', there are writers who continue to assert that men's 'honour' and women's 'shame' play a dominant, decisive role in Andalusian ideology and experience (see, for example, Brandes 1987; Gilmore 1987). I propose that this is an inappropriate paradigm for understanding contemporary Andalusian definitions of gender, sexual behaviour, or morality. Instead I favour an appreciation of the multiplicity and subjectivity that characterise the different criteria upon which reputation is built and judged.

In the ethnography of Andalusia the honour/shame debate was initiated by Pitt-Rivers according to whom, 'The quintessence of manliness [in Andalusia] is fearlessness, readiness to defend one's own pride and that of one's family.' Stressing a connection between sex and gender he continued to assert that, 'It is ascribed directly to a physical origin and the idiom in which it is expressed is frankly physiological. To be masculine is to have *cojones* [testicles]' (1963: 89). He defined this honourable masculinity as a 'moral quality intimately connected with manliness' (ibid.: 91), in relation to which he identified 'The feminine counterpart of the conception, which expresses the essence of womanhood, is *verguenza*, or shame' (ibid.: 111). According to Pitt-Rivers, shame 'is closely associated with sex' and the status of the family depends on women's sexual comportment. His model allocated men and women distinct and separate roles: 'men are entrusted with authority, with the earning of money, the acquisition of prestige' (ibid.: 120) and 'women are entrusted with the maintenance of the home and all that it means' (ibid.: 121). Pitt-Rivers's construction of gender difference has been widely questioned on the basis of later ethnographic work (for example, Corbin and Corbin 1984, 1986; Lever 1986). MacClancey has suggested that Pitt-Rivers's stress on male prestige was informed by a perspective which reflected the dominant Franquist ideology. He observes out that Pitt-Rivers appears to have 'transmitted the views of those males in a structurally similar position to himself', at the expense of the standpoints of others who 'might merely have paid lip service to the values of the dominant group while holding very different views themselves' (MacClancey 1996: 79). There were evidently, as MacClancey demonstrates (ibid.: 80–1), multiple (including 'feminist') perspectives on gender during the Franquist era.

Gilmore's critique of Pitt-Rivers took a different direction, suggesting that Pitt-Rivers had confused 'honor with the more general and inclusive concept of *fama* (reputation, literally fame)'. Gilmore redefined honour as 'sexual vigilance in a predatory environment, in which women are targets and men victims by sexual proxy' (1987a: 127), thereby shifting his emphasis to 'machismo' which he defines as: 'the Andalusian cult of masculinity' (ibid.: 128–9). Gilmore contends that honour and/or reputation are not merely contingent on sexual conduct but also on economic success, honesty, integrity, hospitality and generosity (1987c: 90–1). But whilst he maintains that these are valued as specifically masculine attributes, in my experience of contemporary Córdoba, women are also respected for manifesting such qualities, just as they were in Ronda in the 1970s (as I was informed by John and Marie Corbin). Gilmore's criteria are not exclusive to male reputation, and I believe that he was mistaken to treat it as if it were.[7] In addition, his insistence that a woman's 'shame' and hence a man's 'honour' were contingent on a woman's chastity becomes quite redundant in a situation where women's chastity may be valued and made meaningful from a variety of different and possibly conflicting standpoints. Reputations can change in different contexts, as they are subjectively defined in relation to different discourses. The interface between sexual (or other) behaviour, reputation and subjectivity will produce a variety of different assessments of the status of the same woman, as we saw earlier in the example of Antoñita in the Prologue. Moreover, in Córdoba the term honour seems to be virtually obsolete: the terms *formal*,[8] *legal*[9] or simply *buena persona*[10] were used to express approval during my fieldwork.

## Machismo and Machistas

Gilmore's claim that a cult of machismo is part of Andalusian experience and social order entails a construction of masculinity to which femininity appears incidental. In his theory and ethnography he thus creates a hierarchy that subjugated women to men. It is not surprising this leads him to conclude that 'machismo sustains the society as it is' (1987a: 149). I propose that the term machismo is of 'Gilmorian' rather than Andalusian origin.[11] It neither denotes an Andalusian 'cult of masculinity', nor does it represent a dominant conservative force capable of inhibiting change. My few informants who were familiar with the term associated it with an 'ugly' set of values which were demonstrated by some men and which were insulting to women.

Gilmore justified exchanging the term 'honour' for 'masculinity' on the basis that, 'In modern Andalusia, if you refer to a man's honor, men will laugh or they will direct you to the classic morality plays' (1987a: 129). I doubt very much that they would have found the term *masculinidad* any more relevant. However, I do not want to dispute Gilmore's terminology so much as the 'Andalusian' meanings he allocates to it. In the Córdoba of the 1990s many (especially, but not exclusively) young people (quite apart from defining honour as a redundant term) laughed at the model of sexual behaviour that Gilmore labelled Andalusian masculinity. They attributed such thought and behaviour to very 'traditional' and 'uneducated' people who had spent all their lives in small villages.[12] Gilmore seems wrong to have spoken in general terms of either 'modern Andalusia' or 'Andalusians'; his descriptions represent what some of my informants labelled traditional or anachronistic Andalusian thought. I think Gilmore was very mistaken to assume that such attitudes prevailed as *the* dominant discourse or code in the late 1980s. His continued assertion of this argument in the 1990s is most problematic (for example, Gilmore 1992).[13]

It is surprising that during his fieldwork Gilmore seems to have been unaware of the diversity of sexual experimentation practised by many people. Although most data I collected for the 1970s and 1980s related to long-term heterosexual relationships or casual sex amongst teenagers, some sexual orgies were mentioned. Even if these activities were not practised amongst Gilmore's male working-class informants, and would have been considered immoral by the majority of Andalusian villagers (and urbanites) in the 1970s, they should not be ignored. Such themes were also well represented in the popular culture of the period in film, print and music. Indeed the 1970s and 1980s are often reflected upon as the liberalising era which brought about a sexualisation of popular culture.

Many informants stated that they live in a society which is machista, but they referred to the negative connotations of this condition. An Andalusian woman friend and I spent some time discussing the meaning of the word. Our conclusion was that in general terms it best referred to our understandings of the English term 'sexist'. More specifically, the meaning of machista varies according to which discourse it refers to. For some it meant any situation where women appeared disadvantaged. In contrast, so-called traditionally minded men invoke curious examples to prove that they are not machista; in the words of one informant: 'I'm not machista – I sometimes help my wife lay the table'. Some younger men represented their backgrounds as machista. They said that they personally disliked sexist behaviour, but probably inadvertently displayed sexist attitudes that originated in their 'upbringing'. Women who had moved to Córdoba from other Spanish regions remembered being quite amazed by what they had regarded as a machista Andalusian culture. These representations of local identities also situated Andalusia in national and global contexts. Some informants apologetically compared their local culture negatively to other parts of Spain and Europe. Andalusians sometimes attributed the machista elements of their regional identity to the region's past association with Islamic and Arabic cultures. They associated extreme sexism with southern Mediterranean cultures and explained

Andalusian sexism as the cultural heritage of the historical period during which they were ruled by the Arabic Caliphate. Being a machista was also, by some Andalusians (in their statement of racial difference), endowed with values they associated with stereotypes of north African masculinity.

## Sex in the City?

Gilmore quotes a conversation in which some of his male informants stated that: 'A man and a woman cannot be friends unless the woman is very very ugly and the man is very, very foolish.' A comment that he interprets as follows:

> it is the very nature of the male animal to take advantage of women, to seduce them at every opportunity, to make conquests. A man who fails to heed the call of nature in this respect is weak in his manhood, inferior and foolish. (1987a: 129)

Gilmore thus emasculates many of my informants under the age of thirty. Exclusively male or female peer–groups, or *pandillas,* are normal in Andalusia; however, neither all pandillas nor all close friendships are single sex.[14] In particular, strong friendships between men and women were regarded as normal amongst people in their twenties and thirties. Men who attempted to conquest or seduce women at every opportunity were often seen as irritating and foolish. Some attributed the behaviour of men who tried to have sex with women, without first establishing 'social' relations, to shyness and an inability to relate 'normally' to women. In mixed friendship groups of young middle-class people such behaviour is often seen as problematic and out of place.

Clashes between traditional discourses and different ways of conducting relationships did come into play in the lives of my informants. For instance, gossip networks sometimes made friendships between men and women problematic. References to traditional discourse may be used in gossip strategies even if those participating in the gossip discourse recognise that the connection between the assumptions they employ and the situation to which they apply them is tenuous. One informant was particularly distressed by gossip which all began when she started walking to a government office to check employment information. A young man of her age who lived near by regularly checked the same noticeboard for his sister, so they frequently walked and chatted together. Several of the girl's acquaintances saw them together, amongst whom was a cousin who told family and friends that my informant had a boyfriend,[15] with whom she regularly walked in the street. My informant was most annoyed by this gossip, and her friends and family began jokingly accusing her of having a boyfriend but being reluctant to admit it. Neither she nor her companion were interested in beginning an amorous relationship, and she had to work hard to dissipate all the rumours. She commented that she found the gossip particularly distressing because, as she had no boyfriend, the insinuation that she was almost engaged considerably reduced her chances of meeting one within the circle of her friends which was affected by this rumour.

Gilmore's insistence that 'Andalusian man' and his behaviour are characterised by unquestioned sexual predation seems unwarranted. Whilst some men make comments to some women in the street (it happened to me, and I expect it happens to many women in Andalusia[16]) this is by no means universally considered normal or acceptable.[17] Such behaviour is normally restricted to the occasional comment made in passing, by a man to a woman. Some women ignore these, others are insulted. One young man of about twenty years old, who belonged to an all-male pandilla of guys of his own age regarded himself as being in a trap with respect to meeting women. Being too shy to initiate 'normal' conversation with an attractive girl he stayed in his group, but felt embarrassed by the piropos[18] that some of his friends shouted to girls who passed them in the street. He felt that such behaviour would not help any of the group to meet girls, it was a strategy more likely to alienate girls and thereby reduce his chance of a relationship.

Gilmore argues that in Andalusia it is important that men should be macho: 'Being macho in Andalusia is being sexually aggressive, using only the penis as a weapon' (1987a: 132). He claims that the term macho is used to refer to sexual prowess as opposed to aggression against other men or physical violence against women. In order to stress the sexual meaning of macho Gilmore quotes an informant: '"A macho", one man declared dreamily, "is a man who would make love to a shovel if you put a dress on it"' (ibid.: 132). In Córdoba in the 1990s many people would call such a man an idiot, not a macho. Indeed the only time I heard the term macho in everyday use was with reference to animals and electrical equipment.[19] Equally inapplicable for Córdoba, is Gilmore's informants' belief that there is a very strong danger of sexual intercourse taking place between any man and woman (regardless of their ages) who are left together unchaperoned (ibid.: 132). All men are simply not constantly sexually predatory in this way. I discovered that many Andalusian men would find Gilmore's macho's behaviour unpleasant and irritating. During my research one young man behaved in a way comparable to that which Gilmore describes, 'his sexual impulses were uncontrollable; he cannot be friendly to any woman unless she is ugly, deformed, or bespoken... The macho youth thinks about women with his balls, he thinks with his testicles' (1987a: 133). His aggressive sexuality was considered to be bad behaviour he was thrown out of a night-club. One male informant described such sexual behaviour as a sign of immaturity and a failure to relate to women as 'people'. He saw this as unacceptable, rather than appropriate male behaviour and recalled some examples of how friends of his had acted in the same way in their late teenage years but later modified their behaviour as they became older.

I find Gilmore's interpretation of femininity equally problematic. Basing his analysis on his informants' approval of the passive sexual role played by a woman in a folk-song, he constructs 'ideal' sexual relations as follows:

> The virginal girl may be hot, to use the favoured Andalusian expression, but she has no idea about sex... The male must play the role of the aggressor; he must show the woman her role through instruction tantamount to rape. He must awaken her sexuality through aggressive coercion, penetration, and ejaculation. (1987a: 139)

Whilst commenting that this 'probably reflects a universal narcissistic male fantasy of the willing rape victim', Gilmore disassociates the model from fantasy by maintaining that it is a correct definition of men's and women's sexual behaviour (ibid.). I find Gilmore's assertion that proper sex is analogous or 'tantamount to' rape to be utterly inappropriate. Rape is a very different and serious issue, and Gilmore's failure to distinguish between it and other forms of behaviour is extremely unfortunate. The willing rape victim is indeed a fantasy; rape victims, by my definition, are never willing. It may be true that some men idealise passive, submissive, female sexual behaviour as desirable and appropriate but others have different preferences. However, bar-room conversations about a few bawdy folkloric songs do not provide an adequate summary of Andalusian thought on rape and women's sexual awakening.

Moreover, Gilmore's 'Andalusian view of sexuality' (ibid.: 137) is oblivious to a feminine perspective. His interpretation sets the scene for a very problematic understanding of the grounds upon which women's reputations are lost or maintained in Andalusia.

## Inequalities in Sexual Relations: the smoothing out of double standards?

Gilmore's starting point is an assertion that, 'The seduced woman is diminished: her reputation and her future prospects are destroyed; she becomes damaged goods' (1987a: 134). Whilst this 'double standard' is referred to in Andalusian culture, it is a debated point, not a dominant influential ideology. My partner, an Andalusian, who at the time of my research was in his late twenties, became involved in a series of conversations with a colleague, a man in his sixties, who lacked a formal education and who lived in the small village where we were temporarily based. He felt that my partner had taken on a big responsibility by living with me out of wedlock. He argued that, were the relationship to end, I would have no marriage prospects and would therefore be effectively ruined for life. Their conversations continued over several weeks; my partner never succeeded in convincing his colleague that if our relationship terminated I would recover with my reputation intact and have no problem beginning a new relationship. Neither did his colleague convince my partner of the gravity of our situation. This type of discourse is commonplace between the old and young; both moralities pertain to Andalusian culture and are sometimes pitted against each other in real conflict. Some parents claim to be unaware that their unmarried, late teenage children have active sex lives. Some men and women believe that a woman should be a virgin when she marries. The parents of a young man who was cohabiting with a single mother, voiced their disapproval of the relationship because she had 'been with other men'. In this case her sexual experience was evidenced by her child. Male informants in their twenties responded by pointing out that many women of their age have had a similar degree of sexual experience, but since they had not become pregnant this was not immediately evident.

Models which prescribe women's chastity exist amongst, and are in competition with, a variety of other models for sexual morality in contemporary Andalusia. The male bias in the ethnography of Andalusia has led to an over-emphasis on women's chastity in terms of both ideology and experience – 'many ethnographies of the

Mediterranean and middle east report on an obsession with women's virginity which amounts to a kind of fetishism' (Lindisfarne 1994: 84). It is likely that these reports of women's chastity reflect selective discourses rather than feminine experience. Most informants under thirty in Córdoba thought that the majority of young people were sexually active and that even those who did not admit it or talk about it had some sexual experience. In short, having a girlfriend or boyfriend implied involvement in sexual relations. As one female informant put it, 'I am free to have sex with anyone I like and when I like, and it has nothing to do with what anyone else thinks.' However, it would be unfair to say that these opinions, expressed by perhaps more outspoken informants, reflected a universal feminine experience. Young women may chose to remain virgins for personal or religious reasons, or may simply not find the opportunity to have sex with an appropriate partner. Some do fear that they will, as Gilmore puts it 'lose their reputation' (1987a: 134) or at least their self-respect, and in certain social and cultural circles this may well be their experience. Conservative catholic and religious organisations such as *Opus Dei* have some influence over their members' sexual morality, but religious control of sexuality generally cannot be assumed and State control over sexuality has certainly decreased. In the 1990s women are free to determine their own attitudes to sex and are aware of a variety of alternative sexual moralities. Women are taking control of their own bodies and sexualities in several ways, an important example of which is the use of birth control (see Chapter 7). Indeed chastity itself was also explicitly being redefined in the early 1990s as the international phenomenon of 'Chastity Clubs' caught on in Andalusian cities such as Granada, Seville and Almeria (Tremlet 1994: 3). Some media representations identified these clubs as perverse and pornographic, whilst members claim that the chastity movement is a response to a situation in which they feel under great social pressure to experiment with sex. This phenomenon identifies the women's chastity described in the existing ethnography as something almost marginalised in mainstream urban culture. The new chastity which was being publicly announced and debated during my fieldwork was part of a morality that potentially affects both men and women equally, and it was not specifically or institutionally related to the Catholic church. This version of chastity, unlike traditional women's chastity was not a passive submission to social conventions, rather, it represented a public statement of a notion that both men and women have the right to control their own bodies and sexualities.

The 'fiercely double standard' in which 'the girl stands to lose' and 'He wins a conquest; she loses her reputation' (Gilmore 1987a: 134), loses its significance when it is translated to a contemporary situation in which the site for male conquest is rapidly diminishing and the girl may lose nothing because her reputation is not necessarily related to her virginity. As Gil Calvo puts it, young women today 'in order that they should not lose out, strategically cultivate their best virtue, which in the present is not their virginity, but academic success' (1993: 21). Gil Calvo's observation can be regarded as an unwarranted generalisation,[20] but his point is crucial: a woman's reputation need not be based in her virginity, nor indeed in her sexual conduct. As my partner had tried to point out to his colleague, I was going to get a PhD and would have no trouble finding my way in the world were we to split up. Correspondingly, neither is a man's reputation, masculinity, honour, or whatever one chooses to call it, bound up in the sexual behaviour of the women connected to him by kinship.

In contemporary Andalusia reputation and prestige are not measured according to universal criteria concerning sexual behaviour. Different groups of consensus refer to different models of sexual behaviour. Young people must appear to live up to not one, but several, ideal models of sexual behaviour; in different contexts different people must be convinced of the sexual identity one projects. A young woman may express her sexuality to her parents, boyfriend, lover and close woman friends (and if she is a woman bullfighter, also her public) in very different ways. To understand how women gain prestige it is necessary to refer to other domains of activity, one of which is explored below – the world of 'work'.

## Women's Places, Market Places and Job Markets

In general terms the statistics[21] for the late 1980s and early 1990s indicate increasing employment opportunities for women. Attitudes towards women's work appear more favourable than in the past, and their competition with men in the public work-force seems less problematic to some extent. Ironically, the 'economic crisis' and a restructuring of the labour market have restricted the opportunities which are available in the 1990s. In Andalusia the combination of an acute scarcity of employment and the majority of employment contracts on offer being very short-term, presents great difficulties for many young men and women hoping to gain a permanent foothold in any career (see Pink 1997c, where this situation is discussed in some detail).[22] Other statistical research has suggested that young women are beginning to follow careers that have previously been considered 'typically' masculine (see Gil Calvo 1993). The novelty status of this situation is also stressed in weekend newspaper and magazine reports on, for instance, women fire-fighters, women soldiers and of course women bullfighters. The aspirations of some of my female informants in their late teens and early twenties were to become air pilots, journalists, judges, teachers, university lecturers and anthropologists. This is not to say that many others did not aspire to become wives, mothers or socialites. An appreciation of the diversity of expectations and aspirations represented by the perspectives of Andalusian school-leavers in the 1990s is essential for understanding the very uneven design of the contemporary tapestry of Andalusian gendered identities. Women's participation as firefighters, medical doctors, judges and company directors is lauded by the media, debated in the domestic contexts in which television is viewed and magazines read, discussed in peer-groups and criticised by some traditionalists. It is therefore useful to consider the range of different values against which women's achievements, prestige and reputations may be measured. Prestige is not something that one gains and carries with oneself, rather it is granted anew by different criteria in each situation. A woman who wants to be a bullfighter may be highly respected by some colleagues and her trainer, ridiculed by some of the men against whom she competes, considered foolish by her family, placed on a pedestal by one media camp and harshly criticised by another. My under-standing of the contemporary popularity of women bullfighters rejects anthropological models of one Andalusian gender system that maintains social order by allocating reputation and prestige in relation to masculine honour and feminine shame.

Andalusian gender ideologies do not categorically render women bullfighters unnatural, inappropriate, or morally wrong. In con-temporary Andalusia many people see women's control of their own sexualities, bodies, careers and achievements to be the 'proper' state of affairs. Therefore it seems sensible to argue that, from certain standpoints, a bullfighting career is deemed a perfectly correct, reputable and prestigious route for a young woman to follow.

# Notes

1. See, for example, Connell 1995; Howell and Melhuus 1993; Moore 1993; Stolke 1993.

2. See, for example Broch-Due and Rudie 1993; Connell 1987, 1995; Cornwall and Lindisfarne 1994; Featherstone et al. 1991; Moore 1994; Scott and Morgan 1993; Shilling 1993; Strathern 1988, 1993.

3. Kulick (1995) draws together ideas from feminist theory and anthropology to stress the fragility and instability of identity; in this particular instance to argue that the 'autonomous' self is challenged through sexual intimacy.

4. Loizos notes that since Brandes spent much of his earlier period of fieldwork in an exclusively male bar, 'We might suppose that what men say about women in such contexts has a rather special character, and perhaps an especially negative character', and 'it seems reasonable to wonder how far the views of his male informants about women were decisively shaped by compelling material from those early months of bar-talk' (1992: 174).

5. It is notable that neither representation takes on the discourse about single parenthood.

6. See, for example, Broch-Due et al. (eds.) 1993; Connell 1987, 1995; Cornwall and Lindisfarne (eds.) 1994; de Valle (ed.) 1993; Moore 1994.

7. Pitt-Rivers (1961); Corbin & Corbin (1986); and Brandes (1987) show that shame is not exclusive to women, but they do maintain that it is specifically related to female sexuality.

8. 'Formal', when applied to a person, may be translated as: reliable, dependable, businesslike.

9. 'Legal', when applied to a person, may be translated as: trustworthy, truthful, loyal and reliable.

10. 'Buena', when applied to a person, may be translated as: good, kind, reliable and trustworthy.

11. John Corbin (in personal communication) points out that in Ronda in the 1960s and 1970s the term 'machismo' did not figure in the vocabulary. In Córdoba even in the 1990s the term was not in frequent use, although most younger informants said they understood it. The term machista was applied rather than machismo. Gilmore appears to confuse anthropological theory with Andalusian culture: machismo as an anthropological construct may be useful; as an Andalusian concept it is not relevant.

12. Educated young Italians have also expressed similar perspectives.

13. Vale de Almeida shows how 'predatory' masculinity is lived out in a Portuguese town (for example, 1996: 33–59). However, his interpretation also recognises that whilst gender-relations may be interpreted in terms of a local discourse of male cunning, other urban and feminine understandings of the same specific gender-relations may be different.

14. Uhl reports that in Escalona, an Andalusian village, in the 1980s there

were large mixed-sex pandillas of around thirty pre-courtship youths. Corbin and Corbin also observe that in Ronda mixed-sex pandillas existed, but note that this phenomenon varied according to social class (1984: 79–80).

15. She used the Spanish term *novio* which implies a quite serious boyfriend and possibly an engagement.

16. Similar comments are shouted to women bullfighters when they perform in public. The behaviour of those who make crude remarks about a woman bullfighter's bum is not universally admired nor is it considered appropriate masculine behaviour.

17. For example, one lunchtime I was followed home from the university by a male student who tried to insist on buying me a beer; I managed to deter him after refusing his offer for over ten minutes. When I described his actions, his persistence, and the way he explained his behaviour: 'when you see a pretty girl you naturally want to take her for a drink', to informants of my age they defined his actions as silly, out-of-place and amusing. In short they saw him an object to be laughed about. They did not regard this as the normal male behaviour that Gilmore's model would imply, rather they assessed it as ridiculous and inappropriate. However, it is important not to play down the amount of attention that both men and women pay to one another's appearance both in the street as casual passers-by and in conversations.

18. A piropo is a provocative flirtatious comment, usually made by a man to a woman.

19. Not only is Gilmore's model of masculinity problematic, I believe that he also misinterprets the meaning of the term macho in Andalusian culture (cf. Corbin and Corbin 1986; Hart 1994: 50). In Spanish, the term macho denotes the 'male sex' (cf. Corbin and Corbin 1986; Cornwall and Lindisfarne 1994). Informants insisted that *macho* (male) and *hembra* (female) referred to animals and never to humans. The only other time I heard the term used to refer to sex/gender was in conversations about plug sockets in which macho refers to plug and hembra to socket.

20. The 'double standard' is still alive but not flourishing (see, for example, Orgaz Romero 1992: 74–6). Some informants had an awareness of the double standard which also entailed its critique. This self-criticism represents a process of change, but is not practised by all Andalusians.

21. From 1987 to 1990, whilst there was a 29 per cent increase in the number of women in employment, the increase for men was only 7.9 per cent. The greatest expansion has been amongst married women (Cousins 1994: 48). In Andalusia the percentage of women working is usually lower than that for the rest of Spain; in Andalusia in 1993, 31 per cent of women were active in the workplace (ibid.: 51).

22. Since the 1980s 'temporary fixed-term contract work has become overwhelmingly important as a new form of work' in Spain. In 1991 virtually all new jobs created were occupied by non-permanent employees, and in 1992 31 per cent of men and 39 per cent of women were on temporary

contracts (Cousins 1994: 53). The situation differs according to gender: the number of permanent jobs occupied by men decreased and were replaced by temporary-contract work, whilst 94.5 per cent of the increase in women's employment was in temporary-contract jobs (ibid.: 54). Women have entered the labour market predominantly as temporary-contract workers; many of the jobs available to young people seeking work are offered on the basis of a six- or three-month contract which terminates in a return to unemployment. My informants continually emphasised this problem.

# Gender, Bullfighting and Anthropology: Theorising Women Bullfighters

**T**wo main themes have dominated social-science treatments of the bullfight. In anthropological accounts the performance tends to be represented as a 'symbolic ritual'. As such, the task anthropologists have set themselves is to unravel its message or 'meaning'. Psychological interpretations have been more intent on defining the 'character type' of the bullfighter. Gender has been an indispensable side-show to both these pursuits since their theoretical frameworks depend on the male sex and masculine gender of the bullfighter. The historical developments of the psychological and anthropological approaches have not been entirely independent. For instance, Conrad's (1959: 185) interpretation of the bullfight as 'displaced aggression against the bull as a symbol *par excellence* of power and authority', reappears in some later works (for example, Mitchell 1991). The notion of machismo, that later became central to Gilmore's anthropology (see Chapter 1) was defined by Ingham as a 'defense against homosexual impulses' (1964: 97). He argued that the symbolism of the performance plays out a conflict between homosexuality and heterosexuality. In common with Pitt-Rivers and Douglass, Ingham claimed that the bullfighter becomes increasingly masculine as the performance proceeds and 'the bull is made feminine in the act of dying' (1964: 98). In my opinion these bodies of literature have two problematic themes in common. First, they exhibit a tendency to orientalise both the bullfight and Spanish culture. Second, they offer a static, fixed and supposedly 'objective' view of the relationship between the bullfight, ritual performance and 'culture'. They admit neither women bullfighters nor subjectivity, and do not allow for the continuous creation of culture and invention of meanings.

47

## Anthropological Sacrifice and the Writing of Ritual

Anthropological interpretations have predominantly interpreted the live bullfight as ritual. Pitt-Rivers (1984, 1993, 1995); Douglass (1984); Corbin and Corbin (1986); and Marvin (1988) have proposed the most coherent definitions. Pitt-Rivers (1984, 1993), followed by a series of Spanish anthropologists (Cardín, 1991; Delgado Ruíz 1989; Romero de Solís, 1992, 1995) defines the bullfight as a 'ritual sacrifice', a sacrificial exchange (Pitt-Rivers 1984: 29), a symbolic language, which has survived in 'rational' modern society. Pitt-Rivers, with reference to Turner, regards ritual as better 'read' or understood by an outside observer. He appreciates that symbols are 'polysemic' but assumes the fixity of meaning within cultural or temporal boundaries (1984: 30–1). It seems that Pitt-River's 'objective' anthropological interpretation of the relationship of the bullfight to a homogeneous Spanish culture is unfounded: his reading of the bullfight appears to be no more true than Spanish culture is homogeneous.

According to Pitt-Rivers's (1984) interpretation, the bullfighter begins the performance playing a symbolically feminine role. During the bullfight he becomes increasingly masculine and finally kills the bull as a 'superhero' who violates the taboo of raping a menstruating woman (who is apparently now symbolised by the bull which Pitt-Rivers claims is transformed into a metaphorical female). Cambria has aptly criticised Pitt-Rivers for extracting 'certain aspects from the bullfight (which he confesses, he used to frequent . . . thirty years ago)', imposing a 'sexual/religious interpretation' on them and then applying 'them to Andalusian men and the relations between the sexes in that southern region of Spain' (1991: 221). Yet Pitt-Rivers, apparently oblivious to his critics, has more recently claimed that, 'According to the majority of our anthropologist colleagues of today, the bullfight should be recognised as a sacrifice' (1995: 181).

Douglass (1984) also compares the kill to copulation and has suffered similar criticism (Cambria 1991: 221–2). Douglass extends her analysis to the media:

> Television in Spain now shows bullfights regularly and repeated instant replays of the kill are shown: the torero's blade goes in and out and in and out, for all to see; a kind of televised copulation. (1984: 254)

This emphasis on the repeated 'in and out' (slow) motion of the sword is inappropriate: this kind of action does not dominate televised bullfights. The kill is a key moment in both live and televised bullfights. It is considered by aficionados to be the action that requires most skill and precision, as well as the moment in which the performer is in greatest danger. Slow-motion action replays provide viewers with opportunities to scrutinise and evaluate this important moment. In my experience, when viewing a televised kill aficionados concentrate on technique; a slow-motion kill can become a critical moment, and a dangerous stage in the drama of televised performance. In this sense the televised kill constitutes not a sexual metaphor but a fragment of a media event. Numerous (anthropological and popular) interpretations of the bullfight bear witness to the idea that the performance can become a symbolic representation of human sexuality, but that it is only understood on these terms when sexual meanings are invested in it. The bullfight itself does not essentially symbolise copulation any more than copulation stands for the bullfight.[1] Anthropological readings of supposed pre-existing symbols of the bullfight render it meaningful in terms more significant for their own authors than for the culture as a whole (cf. Fabian 1983: 125). Similarly, classification of the bullfight and other so-called Spanish traditions as uncivilised and irrational throwbacks to pre-Enlightenment Europe (Douglass 1992; Mitchell 1991) constitutes a selective 'othering' of certain aspects of Spanish culture which renders them uncivilised or primitive. Both of these designations are inappropriate: 'there are different cultural definitions of being human, being male and being civilised' (Marvin 1986: 135). The Anglo-Saxon/Spanish distinction represents an example of such variation. Moreover, multiple definitions of being human, male and civilised exist within as well as between cultures. Anthropological definitions of the bullfight as a 'primitive' ritual represent anthropology's (former) preoccupation with the 'classification of primitive social types' (Friedman 1994: 6). By claiming to reveal the non-civilised rationality of other cultures such interpretations support ethnocentric impositions of symbolic meaning. They do not explain its social significance.

Of the non-ethnographic treatments of the bullfight I believe Mitchell's (1991) work to be the most problematic.[2] Mitchell takes up a quest to identify the psychological profile of the bullfighter. To his credit he succinctly criticises Pitt-Rivers's and Douglass's interpretations of the relationship between the bullfight and sex. He points out that, 'Once we jettison empiricism, our answers to the questions "What does bullfighting have to do with sex?" will be limited only by our imagination or our shame' (Mitchell 1991: 155).

Ironically, Mitchell's own brand of empiricism leads him to encounter similar limitations. His own construction of the 'experienced' bullfight could be labelled 'sexual fantasy'; it is certainly not derived from the imaginations of audience members. Mitchell relieves bullfight spectators of their agency and subjectivity to assert that 'an "inherent" relationship between the bullfight spectacle and sex must begin not with what bullfight spectators *say* but with what they *do*.' He argues that the bullfight has a 'structural' (rather than metaphorical) similarity with sex, because both are to do with 'physiological arousal'. In these ways he declares his interest in the 'psychosexual aspects of the bullfight' (1991:159). For Mitchell it is the experienced nature of the bullfight, not its symbolic meanings, that explains the way in which Spaniards unknowingly relate to it. I was surprised (and potentially embarrassed) to learn that, 'Physiological arousal, whether of a gratifying or guilty variety, is an automatic result of viewing bullfights, since they are transgressive by definition and fully participate in the erotic dynamics of violence. We have already seen enough therefore to justify calling the bullfight pornography – in a purely empirical, not judgemental sense' (Mitchell 1991:171). Mitchell continues, to describe bullfighting as, 'The innocent enjoyment of the national pornography' which 'may well be related to a culture-wide predilection for strong sensations in general', and he proposes that 'bullfighting can only be understood in terms of renewable Spanish legacy of emotional volatility' (ibid.:173). Mitchell's analysis of the 'experienced' bullfight can thus appear as a thinly disguised attempt to generalise about the psychology of the 'Spanish character'. He develops his understanding of the bullfight in terms of his model of a national psychological trait that transcends time and space as it 'return[s] to some heroic realm out of time' (ibid.). For Mitchell the audience is made up of passive recipients of erotic imagery, they react as a faceless mass and for them the experience is universal, not personal or subjective. His bullfighter is an extreme of a certain type: a sado-masochist.

### Dramatic Gender

Other interpretations have been more grounded in ethnography, but do not admit women performers. For Corbin and Corbin the theme of the bullfight is masculinity: 'the bullfight epitomises the specifically male predicament and the means of overcoming it'. It is also analogous to public competitiveness where men are judged in terms 'of relative success in coping with difficulties' (1986: 109). However, as I indicated in the previous chapter, in the 1990s women intellectuals, professionals and politicians, are also admired by many for their problem-solving abilities in the public domain. Women must prove that they are competent to deal with public and professional predicaments as they compete with men in the paid work-place. Thus the model in which one is judged by one's capacity to deal with problems also applies to some contemporary femininities.

Marvin also defines the bullfight as a drama about masculinity and a ritual in Lewis's sense of the term; a drama which provokes an emotional response in the audience and which affects the performer emotionally (1988: 167). Pitt-Rivers has seen the bullfight as 'the ritual revindication of masculinity' (1963: 90) but he regards women bullfighters as compatible with his reading of bullfight symbolism. Marvin, on the other hand, demonstrates how women bullfighters can disrupt the ritual structure of the event. According to Marvin's interpretation of the symbolic statements about masculinity represented in the bullfight, women bullfighters, who are seen by his informants as inappropriate and out of place cannot communicate its message which is 'a statement in dramatic form of what it means to be a human male in this [Andalusian] culture' (1988: 142). The authenticity of the emotional responses provoked in both performer and audience through the bullfight are, according to Marvin, dependent on the biological maleness of the bullfighter. When the performer is female the _ambiente_ (emotionally charged atmosphere)[3] of the bullfight is absent.

The qualities that Marvin describes as essential to being male are, in my experience, also incorporated into contemporary Andalusian constructions of femininity. Marvin agrees with Corbin's point that 'Manliness is thought to have a physiological basis – strength of character is equated with "having balls" . . .' (1978: 4), which he uses to argue that the woman bullfighter who has no testicles presents a problem of classification which results in aficionados denying her femininity (1988: 163). For Marvin's own informants his argument may stand, but amongst Andalusians who admire women for 'having balls' it is less convincing. Many of my informants thought it perfectly normal to say that a woman 'has balls', to mean that she is brave and assertive. The woman bullfighter Cristina Sánchez claims to have metaphorical balls and is nevertheless regarded as a very attractive woman. One male informant astutely commented that whilst it is normal to compliment a woman by saying she has balls, the phrase has its origins in 'our sexist society'. Identity is inevitably gendered, but masculine/feminine need not be related to a male/female sex distinction: 'nothing should be prejudged. Being masculine can involve a range of behaviour which elsewhere would be termed feminine' (Cornwall and Lindisfarne 1994: 15).

Cristina Sánchez is quoted in the *Guardian* (a British newspaper) as claiming to have the balls of a bullfighter. 'I have exactly what the men have,' Sánchez insists, 'even the "balls", with my courage!' (Kirsta 1993). In her assertion that she is as brave as a man Cristina does not find it inappropriate to use the metaphor of cojones to refer to the type of bravery she exhibits. Such bravery is often classified as masculine and there is an apparent contradiction and biological impossibility in a woman's claim to have balls; yet Cristina's statement is not meaningless. The idea that a woman may possess metaphorical balls is applied to other discourses on personal qualities and behaviour in Andalusia. To describe a woman as *cojonuda* is usually a positive evaluation. As a rule, in Spanish female organs are used to symbolise human weaknesses and inadequacies whilst male organs are associated with strength of character and social correctness. However, these terms are not necessarily directly related to masculinity or femininity. The point that women can 'have balls' asserts in everyday terms that the bravery required to  bullfight is not exclusive to men. Nevertheless, the idea that both sexes can possess this particular type of bravery is not a matter of universal consensus in Andalusia; this issue must be categorised as a debate (see Chapter 7). I would argue that whilst Marvin describes the basis upon which some men question the femininity of female performers, it is the case that others regard bullfighting as an appropriate expression of femininity.

In the 1990s many women hold positions of power in business, government, administration and elsewhere. Conversely, the discourse central to Marvin's analysis states that 'Not only should women not be publicly assertive in their dealings with men, they should not be seen to compete with men' (1988: 157). This invites the question, according to whom and in what contexts does this statement apply? In Andalusia, women can and do compete with men in public, and, often win. Moreover, they are frequently admired for doing so. Questions of 'by whom?' and 'in what context?' are also relevant. It is necessary to account for multiple perspectives on femininity and masculinity in order to understand how women performers are conceptualised by bullfight aficionados. For example, some aficionados told me that women should compete in 'women only' events to keep men's and women's bullfighting separate. Several other 'great aficionados' argued that men and women bullfighters should perform together (see Chapter 7). Furthermore, many bullfight aficionados are women (see Chapter 4). The gender stereotypes reiterated in traditional bullfighting discourse and imagery do not necessarily correspond with the way in which men and women conceptualise or live out gender roles in bullfighting social circles. Women are beginning to play increasingly active, decisive, productive and influential roles in the bullfighting world (see Chapters 3 and 4).

## Women in Bullfighting or Women's Bullfighting?

The theoretical assumption that the ritual structure of the bullfight prohibits the acceptance of women bullfighters implies that their performances cannot be defined as 'ritual'. However this model is challenged by the empirical presence of women bullfighters in the ritual which is the bullfight. The contemporary participation of women performers could render invalid anthropological inter-pretations of the bullfight as a ritual about masculinity. Women performers cannot adhere to the 'structure and formal character-istics' (Marvin 1988: 167) of the ritual because they are female. Do women subvert the ritual of the bullfight or do they create a different ritual?

It is useful to interpret rituals as polysemic in a way that neither Turner (1967: 50-1) nor Pitt-Rivers (1984) intended. The bullfight is a visual and emotional performance which may be interpreted subjectively in terms of a variety of models of masculinity and femininity. By stressing differences within cultures a revised agenda may be set. Thus I propose to inquire not into what the symbols say about the culture that produces them, but into the plurality of meanings of the performance for those who participate in it as performers and audience. In general, there is much debate over whether or not women should be bullfighters, and Andalusian aficionado opinion on bullfighting and gender is diverse and multiple. Marvin's interpretation of the bullfight's message as 'what it means to be a human male in this culture' (1988: 142) corresponds with one particular traditional Andalusian masculinity and a binary

*definition of ritual.*

model of gender. I would like to consider the bullfight in a context of multiple masculinities and femininities (cf. Cornwall and Lindisfarne 1994) in order to account for a variety of subject positions.

Of course, this project does not render traditionalist discourse irrelevant. Marvin's point that the atmosphere (ambiente) of the bullfight changes according to the biological sex of the performer is fundamental. Other key issues are: the communication between performer and audience, audience consensus, and the argument that women bullfighters cannot produce the ambiente associated with a good performance because they are biologically female. Therefore, traditionalist perspectives and the lack of audience consensus continue to present practical problems for women performers.

## Performance and Embodied Performers

### Performance as representation

An examination of the ways in which the performance and its ambiente may change when the performer is female reveals much of interest. Firstly, I shall consider the bullfight as a dramatic performance.

Pitt-Rivers has suggested that similarities exist between bullfighting and theatre. He argues that the biological sex of the performers is unimportant and, as in theatre, the gender of performers is interchangeable. This analysis is problematic because Pitt-Rivers bases his understanding of the meaning of women performers solely on his own reading of bullfight symbolism. Moreover, he fails to acknowledge fundamental differences between the bullfight and theatrical productions.

The bullfight is not staged; the difference between the actor and the torero is essential for understanding its emotive atmosphere. As Marvin points out, 'The role of the torero is much more closely tied to the man himself than the role of actor is tied to the person who is an actor.' He continues, 'The torero performs as himself – the role of torero is not thought to be separable from the man who is a torero' (1988: 178–9). In the bullfight mortal danger is real, not evoked as in theatre. The 'emotion and excitement are generated because of the danger' (ibid.: 179). In Marvin's analysis the performer must be male and the drama of the bullfight is part of a wider representation of the life of the bullfighter. He lives out his role not only in the bullring but in his everyday masculine lifestyle. For Marvin this entails an exclusion of female performers. However, many aspects of the drama and experience that Marvin describes as masculine may equally be related to contemporary feminine experience. Many contemporary categories of gendered experience and activity do not correlate with Marvin's definition of masculinity *vis-à-vis* the bullfight. Like any male bullfighter, the woman bullfighter is no actor; the drama of her performance is also about her, the person. Therefore, a woman performer acts herself – a woman who has succeeded in the public sphere and become a bullfighter. Gender roles are contested in contemporary Spain and there is consensus neither in 'the culture' nor amongst bullfight aficionados about the range of roles women should adopt. The bullfight may, for some, represent a model of contemporary femininity.

*Representation and presentation*

I have outlined above how the bullfight may be interpreted as a story that parallels certain models of success in social life. Simultaneously it is an event in which the skill of the individual performer is judged according to a fixed set of criteria. This constitutes a direct presentation[4] of the performer's skill in which art, technique and knowledge are embodied in, and expressed by, human bodies. Women bullfighters act roles *in* not *with* their bodies. In the live bullfight the body of the performer is an experiencing, communicating body; an expressive body (cf. Frank 1991). Some do not accept the female body as the bearer of such masculine accomplishments. For them the equation of female body/feminine self/professional does not add up to one who is a 'bullfighter'. This perspective may be related to the claim of some aficionados, that a woman cannot evoke the ambiente of a 'true' or 'pure' bullfight. In the context of my understanding of gender and experience as embodied, I suggest that the body should be central to a discussion of women bullfighters. This is both relevant to interpretations of the bullfight as a dramatic representation and as a presentation of individual talent. Women's lifecycles in contemporary Spain are diverse and varied. Different women use their bodies in a variety of different ways; and plural models of feminine success coexist. Women bullfighters complete particular personal and professional career plans. Their strategies may involve quite different uses and ways of experiencing their bodies and selves from, for example, women whose life plans prioritise childbearing and mothering.

*research*

In Chapter 7 I shall draw on my ethnography to show how different aficionados and members of audiences understand female bodies in different ways. Some images of the female body, previously marginalised in bullfighting iconography are gaining acceptance as they become dominant symbols in popular culture. Imagery of sportswomen is particularly relevant. Hargreaves points out how, 'Current representations of the female sporting body show some collapse of conventional points of reference, some acceptance of values which have previously been marginalized, and the emergence of new radicalized images of female physicality' (1994: 173). Changing perceptions of women bullfighters' body images may parallel this process as they also become increasingly acceptable when considered in relation to other female body images.

I believe that attempts to define *the* symbolic meaning of woman bullfighters do not represent a valid enterprise. Instead I propose a consideration of why particular different meanings are invested in their iconography. As Strathern points out, 'we should not forget that vision is embodied. In that case, in what kinds of bodies are the eyes set?' (1993: 42). Therefore, with a definition of vision and experience as 'embodied' I propose to focus on how the visual performances of bullfighters' sexed bodies are experienced and made meaningful. In chapter 7 I will explore this question in terms of audience members' interpretations of the performer's physical presence and of the creation of emotion. In Chapter 8 I shall consider similar issues in a discussion of televised bullfights. It is clearly the case that biological sex is important; some members of the audience who are accustomed to seeing a male body performing may find it difficult to identify with the performance of a female body. If they are unable to empathise with a performing female body then the ambiente characteristic of a good professional bullfight may not be forthcoming. Members of the audience identify with differently sexed bodies in different ways and this may be a determining factor in the type of ambiente which they perceive. Audience members may also be aware of a restricted consensus when women perform since their sex remains a problematic issue for a large proportion of the audience.

For many aficionados it is precisely the biological sex of the performer, rather than his/her sexuality, that is at issue. Several bullfighters are thought or known to be homosexual but this does not create an ambiguous category for traditionalist aficionados (cf. Marvin 1988). Neither did I find the homosexuality of bullfighters represented as a media scandal during my fieldwork. Informants and media discourses did not tend to feminise conceptually homosexual bullfighters. There was one instance when a retired bullfighter was said always to have a 'young man' with him, thus indicating that the bullfighter was the senior partner in the relationship, and thereby feminising the 'young man'. However, in my experience, aficionados very infrequently speculated over the homosexuality of performers. Certainly I never heard it suggested that being a homosexual would impede a bullfighter's career. Rather, the physical experience of male sexuality was associated with the experience of bullfighting. For example, some informants told me that bullfighters were believed occasionally to ejaculate during a particularly exhilarating and intense performance. On this physiological basis aficionados could incorporate homosexual men into their perspective upon bullfighting, whilst automatically excluding women[5].

Debates about the nature of women bullfighters' bodies are therefore central to the issue of women bullfighters. In Chapter 7 I discuss how the female body has been considered unsuitable for bullfighting in terms of the composition, 'functions' and 'experience' of a woman's body. Arguments against women performers tend to concentrate on female physiology and to naturalise gender difference. Women bullfighters and their supporters counter their opponents by arguing that they lack reason and evidence. The issue at stake is often one of whether women performers are restricted by their physiology or by their intelligence. Intelligence, emotion and fear are gendered by those who argue that feminine intelligence cannot understand bullfighting. This standpoint implies that minds which are intellectually feminine cannot direct their female bodies as if they were bodies of (male) bullfighters. Successful women bullfighters have been referred to as having the body of a woman but the mind of a (male) bullfighter. Similarly, some would argue that feminine fear combined with feminine intelligence (both elements of a 'normal' female biology) are incapable of correctly judging the bullfight. The body is central to the ways in which performers are believed to internalise, rationalise, and express the bullfight. *the way women interpret fear*

Women performers and women's bullfighting are criticised and evaluated in a range of different discourses and in relation to a variety of points of view. An understanding of how the idea of women in bullfighting is made meaningful requires attention to this multiplicity of perspectives. Standpoints on women's roles in bullfighting can thus be interpreted as participating in a debate that is inevitably related to other cultural discourses. In Chapter 6 I will concentrate on clothing and language to explore the construction of different traditions of bullfighting and the feminisation of performers and performance. In Chapter 8 I shall examine the media context of the success of women bullfighters; and the relationship between live performances and televised bullfights. These represent just some of the narratives into which women performers are incorporated.

# Notes

1. Compare with Frank (1991) who makes similar comments about dance.

2. Mitchell's similar approach to Spanish Flamenco (1994) has also been critically received (Pink 1997f; Washabaugh 1996).

3. The term ambiente (when a positive meaning is intended) is usually used to refer to a lively and social atmosphere and is not limited solely to performances or specific events. It is also used to comment on general atmosphere and, for example, can be applied to a city, or neighbourhood (see Dreissen 1981: 27; Marvin 1988: 129; Murphy 1978: 23). See also Diaz de Rada and Cruces (1994) for a discussion of the term ambiente.

4. I use the term 'presentation' here to emphasise the difference between the bullfighter and actor, and to define the body of the woman bullfighter as distinct from that of the actor. Falk defines the actor's use of his/her body as follows: 'An actor in a play uses his body primarily as a tool, as a means of expression (speech, mime, gestures). The actor uses his body as an instrument in a re-presentation: standing *before* the audience (his concrete presence) but at the same time standing *for* something that is absent, that is his or her "role" in the play' (Falk 1994: 199). The bullfighter's body does not stand *for* absence, it is utterly present and at risk.

5. I did not actively explore the theme of bullfighting and homosexuality during my fieldwork, and found that it was not an area of discussion that often arose whilst I was in Spain. Interestingly, the question has more frequently been raised by anthropologists in response to my work.

# Part 2

# *Detras de la Barerra*? Women off Stage and Women Creeping out from Behind the Scenes

In Chapters 3 and 4 I explore how different discourses on femininity intersect with the world of bullfighting. In this section I will focus on the non-performing roles played by women in the bullfight. I explore representations of traditional masculinities and femininities as they are articulated in both Andalusian discourses and in existing anthropological accounts of the bullfight. I question the existence of parallels between these representations of gender and women's everyday experiences of the bullfight. Instead I propose an approach that investigates how different women weave the bullfight into their everyday lives, lifecycles and careers. Thus I hope to explore how the bullfight is incorporated into a range of different feminine identities and women's activities.

# three

# Wife, Seductress, Mother and the Beautiful Spectator: Representations of Femininities and Tradition

One day when we were discussing the role of women in bull-fighting the Cordoban poet Baldomero Herrero Sánchez de la Puerta presented me with a piece of his unpublished prose. This short work described the experience of a rejoneador who discovered in the audience a woman whom he had wanted to meet for some time. This woman had attended the performance knowing of his desire, and once he had noticed her the rejoneador paid more attention to her teasing eyes than to the dangerous bull he confronted. The piece ends with the performer's arrival at his hotel, where he lights a cigarette and composes the following verse:

Con mi jaca la Trianera,        With my horse, La Trianera,
Le puse un par de castigo,       I punished the bull with my spear,
Sus ojos en la barrera,          Her eyes, at the ringside,
Jugaban igual conmigo.           Toyed equally with me.
Que mi jaca con la fiera.        As my horse did with the beast.

I received accounts of a wide range of roles which women ought to play in the world of bullfighting, yet most people I spoke to tended to agree that the traditional role of women in bullfighting was that of the 'beautiful spectator'. This image was then often used as a reference point against which each speaker could gauge his/her own subjectivity. The author of the piece quoted above presented me his poem precisely as an expression of the feminine role in the bullfight performance. Structurally it locates women in a supportive position in the bullfighting world. Furthermore, it represents women as a part of a functioning whole, allocating them a non-performing

61

role that is an essential complement to the role of the torero. 'Women have an important role to play at the bullfight, but not as performers, rather they have the more emotive role of gracing the audience with their beauty' another middle–aged man told me. He was referring not to the emotional experience of the women themselves as spectators, but to the emotional aesthetic of seeing a beautiful woman adorn the bullring. The poet, in contrast, was quite consistent in his admiration for Cristina Sánchez, and his scorn for those male performers who, in 1993 when she was at novillero level, refused to share the arena with her. It would appear that artists whose creations are built on, and represent, gender difference are not necessarily proponents of an everyday social order organised on the basis of sexual difference. Nevertheless, much art, poetry, photography and oration in bullfighting culture is centred on this traditionalist model that often renders women ornamental spectators, and men triumphant heroes. This gendered imagery is deeply entrenched in the historical iconography of bullfighting culture and is maintained through constant reiteration in oral, visual and performance arts, festivals, and in conversation. It is reified in the material culture of bullfighting, in the posters, photographs, and videos that are the stuff of (often extensive) private collections, and it is also visualised through description. Thus traditional femininity becomes a cultural resource that is invoked, referenced or materially present in both representations of others and expressions of self. Yet this does not imply that the gender role segregation model implied by the traditional imagery prevails as the power base of a hegemonic masculinity. In my experience people tended to construct and identify a traditional femininity against which they would then locate other particular women in moral terms. As I described in the Prologue, Antoñita was set against traditional femininity in a variety of ways, each stressing a different aspect of tradition and each attributing value to different models of femininity: one visualised her as 'ugly'; another invoked the art of Julio Romero de Torres to situate both her and his own integrity; as an English student my eyes saw a young woman wearing a green suit with a motorbike helmet under her arm.

Some, like the poet admitted the traditional discourse as an artistic device in itself, worthy of representation, but not applicable as a universalising moral statement about the roles women should play in bullfighting. It would seem as if women could simultaneously participate in two apparently contradictory discourses. Thus some aficionados encountered no ambiguity between the 'romantic emotional' element of the bullfight and the everyday nature of women's participation. One informant generalised from the romantic discourse that 'a bullfighter needs beautiful women in the audience to inspire him to perform well.' He compared this situation to his own experience: when asked by his friends to bullfight with a small cow at a country festival, he refused to perform until persuaded by a pretty woman. For this man the romantic and flirtatious elements were essential to the bullfight, they demanded that a woman perform the role of spectator so that he could perform the role of bullfighter. Yet this informant's story is very different to a statement that all women are categorically spectators; he also maintained that women and men were equally capable of becoming accomplished bullfighters and should be respected on an equal basis. I found that many men, when questioned about the role of women in bullfighting supported and praised Cristina Sánchez and were comfortable with the idea that women should be bull breeders, the managers of bullfighters, and the organisers of all kinds of taurine events. At the same time, these men in their roles as journalists, artists, photographers, writers or simply speakers were often active in the representation of traditional gender difference. They were perfectly comfortable switching between these (apparently contradictory) narratives. This coexistence of traditional and other strands of thought in individual subjectivities as well as in what we may call bullfighting culture is, as I shall argue in Chapter 8, fundamental to the contemporary status of the bullfight in a consumer society. Others, in contrast, could not accept such ambiguity between feminine identities, women's activities and experience, and the iconography of tradition. Demanding that the only place a woman may take in the bullring is in the audience, these commentators frequently directed me to the 'evidence' of artistic representations of the bullfight and collections of vintage bullfight posters where paintings of women spectators are commonplace. From the latter accounts it would be easy to assume, as other anthropologists have, a direct correlation between 'aficionado opinion' and representations of women as aesthetic objects rather than individual subjects. Women, I was told by two older male informants on separate occasions, are not expected to have the 'true' understanding of bullfighting; it is exclusive to the 'male intellect.' Whilst such opinions can easily be elicited from the tongues of Andalusians, they must be taken to represent only one vision of the world – they are neither a fixed empirical reality nor the Andalusian gender order. I end this chapter by exploring some of the ways in which traditional femininity is worked into representations of self and others, and the performance of everyday life in Andalusia. First I will outline the models of femininity that tend to emerge from traditional discourse.

## The 'Women who Pray' . . . and the Women of Prey

'Of course the other image that people talk about is this idea of women who pray' said a young woman *aficionada* with whom I had been discussing attitudes to women in bullfighting. Other informants had mentioned that the bullfighter's mother and wife 'typically' either remained in the chapel or beside the telephone during his performances – the black and white images of the final scenes of the original film version of *Sangre y Arena* flashed through my mind. The ever-loyal wife of Juan the bullfighter is seen praying in the chapel of the bullring as her unfaithful husband steps out to what will surely be his certain death in the arena. The cover of the first Spanish history of women's bullfighting (Boada and Cebolla 1976) has as its front cover a delightful reversal of this image. It takes the form of a painting in which a large woman bullfighter dressed in a suit of lights sits breast-feeding her baby in the chapel, whilst a man, presumably her husband and painted half her size, kneels at the altar in his everyday suit, his hands clasped in prayer. This topsy-turvy microcosm can have various impacts: on the one hand it appears to play on the grotesque and to cry out for the maintenance of a 'gender order', but on the other it depicts a powerful woman, mother and bullfighter. Its meaning is dependent on the viewer and (amongst other things) on that person's position concerning the compatibility of motherhood with a demanding and dangerous career (see Chapter 7).

The beautiful traditional woman is frequently referenced in art, literature and film to represent feminine moral integrity.[1] Her morality coincides with that of two models of 'women who pray': the wife and mother of the bullfighter. The close relationship of ideal wives and mothers to the bullfighter supposes that they form the bedrock and security of his emotional well-being. In novels and film such women are represented mainly in domestic and religious contexts; and their lives are said to be dominated by the suffering caused them by the constant danger which faces their bullfighter

**Figure 8:** Boada and Cebolla's (1976) *Las Señoritas Toreras*

sons or husbands. In opposition to these images stands the model of 'woman as seductress.' In *Sangre y Arena* the role of seductress is played by Doña Sol who seduces and then toys with Juan in such a way that the viewer cannot help but blame her for his death. The seductress rejects the morality inscribed in traditional codes of conduct. She is lost, unconnected, free; her sexuality is uncontrolled and the bullfighter is in constant danger of falling prey to her charms. This image appears frequently in early twentieth-century fiction[2] and film; and during the last twenty years (since 1970) several 'media women' who have become involved with bullfighters have been cast in the same frame (see below). However, parallel to the congruence of this narrative to media women, an analysis of other domains of popular culture indicates that the contemporary meanings invested in the seductress or femme fatale by cultural producers, artists and audiences should be reconsidered. Pels and Crébas's analysis of Bizet's (1845) *Carmen* argues that the femme fatale of mid twentieth-century representations has been redefined in the 1980s by cinéastes (Godard, Saura and Rosi) who have gone back to Bizet's (1845) text to exchange the 'classic icon of the femme fatale' for a 'new feminine icon' (1991: 345). The new Carmen of Saura's film is 'an independent young woman' (ibid.: 344). In this version the negative connotations of the femme fatale are redefined as the markings of feminine strength surrounded by masculine weakness:

> capriciousness and the hunger for power now become self-assurance and sovereign wilfulness; provocativeness becomes self-conscious femininity and expressiveness; whorishness becomes sexual frankness. In this way the *femme fatale* is transformed from a masculine fantasy . . . into a women's fantasy in which the woman can usurp all kinds of 'masculine' characteristics without losing her femininity (1991: 346).

This reading of Saura's *Carmen* shows that gendered identities and the moral weight they carry are not set in stone in the 'classic tale,' yet further research would be required to account for the variety in Andalusian interpretations of the 'new *Carmen*.' I would argue that Carmen may be easily slotted into a range of different readings, and whilst Pels and Crébas identify how a particular standpoint reworks the narrative and its morality, this 'meaning' is not the only possible interpretation of the film. I believe that the question of what type of woman Carmen represents should be related to Andalusian debates around femininity. Saura's work was popular amongst both traditionalist informants and those who criticised tradition. Some of the latter were also interested in the films of Pedro Almodovar, whose leading actor, Antonio Banderas also starred in Saura's film *Dispara* (Shoot) the narrative of which centres on a woman fugitive – a traditionally masculine role. In Almodovar's *Matador* the boundaries between the ritual killing of animals and human murder as well as those between traditional gender roles are transgressed. The femme fatale is a successful woman lawyer, association with whom leads to the death of an ex-bullfighter (who has become a serial killer) and of the woman herself. The seductress or femme fatale thus fits into a range of different moral perspectives on gender relations in a variety of ways.

Nevertheless, the seductress does live on in some people's imaginations as a devilish threat and as a marker against which to judge her less dangerous counterpart: the 'poor misguided' woman – a 'victim' passed around by a string of bullfighters who use her for sex and then quickly tire of her. This woman misunderstands the meaning of *afición* and follows a misguided route in order to become closer to the world of bullfighting. One informant told me the tale of a woman from his village who had employed this strategy in order to become closer to the bullfighting world and in the hope of gaining opportunities to train and practise with live bulls. She had sexual relations with many bullfighters who did not really care for her, but at least she was allowed some chances to practise bull-fighting. Unfortunately one day she was knocked on the head when training with a live bull. She was said to have never recovered from this injury, which resulted in her developing a split personality – 'if one passes her in the street she is just as likely to greet you with a friendly hello as to punch you.' My informant concluded that the woman, by now middle-aged, was a pitiful creature. The relationship between this tale and that woman's actual experience is another matter. However, the concluding interpretation is both curious and revealing: as in fictional accounts of the immoral seductress, the result of non-conformity to one's proper role is the threat of insanity and disorder.

### Passivity, Activity and the Gender Myth

The active man, passive woman dichotomy has been maintained throughout history in various spoken, written and artistic (and anthropological) renderings of gender, and often becomes a reference point in local discourses. In Chapter 1 I argued that some of the existing anthropological literature has tended to cast Andalusian women into a passive role, structurally opposed to active man. As MacClancey (1996) has shown, women in Spain have not always been 'passive' non-actors. For these reasons I suggest a consideration of how women's action, assertion and power is experienced and represented in everyday life.

In Córdoba early twentieth-century local newspapers cast doubt on the universality of the porcelain fragility of the *Mujer Cordobesa*. Reports of working-class-women smashing china plates, fighting, and being arrested for causing public disturbances in the *Corradera* Market Square are by no means representations of silent submission. Gilmore's model of passive or submissive woman is similarly contradicted in representations of upper-class women. Literary accounts in particular have stressed the international and 'foreign' connections of society women in order to criticise their deviant, immoral and above all non-traditional behaviour. Historically, according to Mitchell, another feminine model was related to the bullfighter figure: the *maja* and torero formed a matching pair. The style of a maja was 'bold, sexy, self-assured' (1991: 56) and 'traditional' (see, for example, Gautier 1975). In this equation the maja was placed in opposition to the seductress. Mitchell sees *majismo* as an eighteenth-century folk response to the Enlightenment and Europeanism which was so attractive to the upper classes (1991: 56–7). Mitchell opposes the traditional morality of the 'saucy sexuality' of the maja and torero to the flirtation, experimentation and 'moral decay' of the upper classes (1991: 56–61). In much bullfighting fiction upper–class women with their experience of foreign ideas and objects are portrayed as individualistic, untraditional and immoral seductresses (for example, Blasco Ibañez 1991; Gautier 1975).[3] Doña Sol of the first film version of *Sangre y Arena* has travelled in the Orient, whilst in the most recent production Doña Sol played by Sharon Stone, has been educated in the United States. Different discourses on the foreign threat to traditional morality can thus become intertwined as classic tales are retold in different historical periods. Contemporary readings of these films (which were both screened on Spanish television and in the *Filmoteca* Cinema in Córdoba during my fieldwork) must also account for the ways in which Sharon Stone has been shaped and intrepreted as a 'media woman' in gossip and other film literature. Particularly after her appearance in *Basic Instinct*, a film which was at the centre of much controversy during my fieldwork,[4] and was screened uncensored in

Spain, Sharon Stone was admired by many of my younger informants as were the feminine roles she represented.

Historically and in the 1990s a variety of different femininities are
available for comparison with traditional femininity. However,
traditional femininity is not a constant variable, but a model
subjectively redefined for specific purposes.

## Material Culture and Media Women

In this section I describe in more detail how 'traditional' femininities
are constructed in literature, the media and visual imagery to show
how they are applied to public figures and incorporated into
everyday lives. A study of photographs published in bullfight reports
from the 1950s to the early 1990s[5] reveals a continuing use of an
iconography of general feminine spectator/individual masculine
performer consistent with some historical artistic representations.
Audience shots in particular can be divided into these categories by
which women are represented in relation to men. Titles such as 'A
young aficionada'; 'Two girls from Bilbao', 'César Rincon and Pablo
Copera [two bullfighters] with a female friend'; 'A pretty aficionada'
and 'Pretty faces at the ringside' (Aplausos, 30 August 1993) accompany images of nameless women who adorn both the bullring and
the pages of bullfight magazines, in addition to being focused on by
TV cameras. Today, in the 1990s, the structure of visual bullfight
reports appears to have changed little since the 1970s. Longer visual
sequences include shots of the other key non-performing participants; the critics, bull breeders, managers and ex-bullfighters in the
audience. All are identified as active participants, and most of them
are men (the exception being those women who own and manage
the ganaderías). They are captioned according to the professional role
of the male subject in bullfighting. In contrast, most shots of women
in the audience will bear her name only if she is the relative or lover
of a bullfighter or if she is a dignitary who holds a public office.
Whilst the latter does reflect the growing participation of women in
public domains, its incorporation into the existing format leaves the
reader to make their own decision as to whether he/she finds the
coexistence of different feminine roles in bullfighting on the same
magazine page or TV screen ambiguous. I discussed these page lay-
outs with educated young women who were training for professional
jobs. They agreed with me when I suggested that a gender imbalance
was represented in these pages, but initially they only saw a normal

bullfight report. As I show in the next chapter women's participation in bullfighting does not necessarily attempt a reconfiguration of its material culture.

I discovered that the more famous a woman is in her own right, the more likely she is to be photographed. For example, between 1992 and 1993, Rocío Jurado a popular singer of traditional Spanish music, and the partner of the bullfighter Ortega Cano, was frequently photographed at his performances; when *Finito de Córdoba* began a relationship with the daughter of another bullfighter, Paco Camino, photographic reports of her presence at his performances were published. Two categories of women that informants identified as ideal wives for a bullfighter were singers of traditional Spanish songs and the daughters of an older performer. The publication of photographs such as the ones mentioned above thus refers to traditional patterns. Nevertheless, many readers of the gossip and bullfight media in which these images are published know that they only tell one story. A woman may simultaneously be represented in a traditional narrative and be a student at law school. Similarly, a range of different narratives may be constructed around the same activity. For instance, in Córdoba between 1993 and 1994 the achievements of two young women who had organised a series of bullfights, and a woman who had taken on the management of a bullfighter's career potentially challenged the masculine domination of most of those activities in bullfighting. However, since accounts of their project were published alongside reports of more conventional happenings their activity was 'made safe', thereby allowing those who found them 'out of place' to locate them in a more secure position. Thus, in this context the teenagers' achievements became novelty items; they could be regarded as curious deviations from the norm. Women's involvement in conventionally masculine roles is novel in the sense that it becomes news, whereas a man may perform the same role without publicity. Such news need not be read in only one way – it may be simultaneously understood as insignificant, threatening, or admirable.

## Women who are Spectators

I found that the captioning of audience portrait photography tends to displace the 'feminine subject' and locate her within a traditional gender order. Women who dress and style their hair in ways that allow them to resemble 'beautiful spectators' in visual represent-

**Figure 9:** The bullfighter *Finito de Córdoba* acknowledges the women with whom I attended his performance. Whilst my photography followed a format of woman spectator, man performer, the young women with whom I sat planned to follow careers in Journalism and Aviation.

© Sarah Pink

ations of *feria* bullfights may also aspire to be pilots, journalists, or lawyers. It would seem that visual narratives which use images of women to point to tradition do not necessarily serve to reinforce traditional ideologies. The bullfight photographer's brief requires the acquisition of certain shots, amongst which are audience shots of women[6].

There is no single reason why women go to bullfights. Nor is there a general feminine experience of the performance. Two sisters who previously insisted they were against bullfighting, who considered it cruel and boring, were happy to sit with their family in the most prestigious front-row seats in the arena for a feria bullfight. The bullfight in Spain has an important social dimension and both women and men attend for reasons related to this social element rather than their afición. However, those who are heavily involved in the social world of bullfighting as well as being fervent aficionados, combine the two. The wife of one ex-bullfighter, an aficionada herself, explained that the feria bullfights have a far greater social importance than occasional performances held at other times of the year. I noticed that it was especially during the feria that some women would enact roles which approach that of the 'beautiful spectator.' For example, women of what one woman referred to as the 'higher level' of the social world of bullfighting – the wives, mothers, sisters and daughters of bullfighting celebrities – treat the feria as a crucial date in their social calendar. The feria bullfights signify the start of a social year: the women who mix in this circle purchase their summer wardrobe for the beginning of the Season in Córdoba. The feria bullfight series was thus compared to a fashion parade in which one shows off one's new outfits for the first time. The social element extends beyond the performances which are usually followed by dinners in restaurants and other forms of celebrations. Aficionadas who do not form part of this social circle also feel some pressure to dress appropriately for the feria bullfights. I was told of one woman who had an expensive Cordoban hat handmade so as to wear it with a *traje corto* costume. Many younger women also feel obliged to go to the bullfight dressed in a suit, whilst others dress smartly but in jeans. Others, on this occasion, thought it a pleasant detail to put a flower in one's hair. When one attends the bullfight one performs a particular role in the audience. Different women interpret this role in their own personal style and express it in a variety of different ways – through costume, body movement and speech. The smart suits, rabbitskin hats, flowers and fans can all be interpreted with reference to tradition and they demonstrate how that discourse is intertwined with the bullfight both as it is created and experienced through the subjectivity of audience members. Some women perform their audience role with reference to other conventions: one woman friend with whom I attended the bullfight shouted like the men seated around us; another friend spent the bullfight sighing at the sight of the attractive torero in the ring, delighted when he performed close by our seats. During the bullfights, and throughout the feria to which they ran parallel each woman appeared to be performing in relation to ideas of tradition. One afternoon during the feria I met another friend, she was dressed in her traje corto, the traditional costume that she wore for feria in order to show me the *traje*, both because it would be useful for my research and personally interesting to me (see Figure 10). This friend did not regard herself as being particularly traditional and she was not at all attracted to the bullfight; in fact, she once told me that she had discovered more about the traditional aspects of Andalusian culture by helping to find out things for my research than she had previously been aware of before. Despite this, in showing me her traje she was at the same time performing a generalised representation of tradition. By showing me what women wear for the feria she was simultaneously locating her own subjective use of the costume in this frame. During the feria people enact or perform what it is they think of as tradition; they are not necessarily essentially traditional themselves. This event that is publicly defined as traditional is organised and enacted on a large scale. I do not believe to dress in a traje corto for feria is an essentially traditional activity, rather it seems to entail a represent-ation of contemporary definitions of tradition. Thus, the versions of femininity played out by women in feria and other festivities should not be taken as either inversions or representations of actual everyday power relations between men and women. Instead I feel that the relationship between traditional ritual and festivity and everyday life should be regarded as more complex; it involves an uneven series of links that may be interpreted as inconsistencies, continuities, inversions and parallels. As I have argued in an analysis of the *Becerrada Homenaje a la Mujer Cordobesa*, which is a 'women only' bullfight held at the end of the feria season in Córdoba, such enactments of tradition do not mirror society, social structure or gender relations, rather they play out those narratives which are commonly thought of as traditional (Pink 1997b)[7]. The sisters whom

**Figure 10:** Encarni is an English teacher in a FE college in Spain. She has no interest in bullfighting and does not lead what she considers to be a 'traditional' lifestyle. However she is interested in some traditional music and dance and dresses in her *traje corto* for the *feria*. One day during *feria* she dressed in her *traje* so that I may see her 'traditional' costume and photograph her. Most other informants who saw this image remarked that she looked like a 'typical', 'traditional' *Cordobesa*.
© Sarah Pink

I discussed at the beginning of this section often complained of the tedium of their father's obsession with bullfighting, but they expressed themselves very differently when seated at the ringside. Just as tradition may be performed during feria or for the bullfight, it is also enacted during the course of everyday life – it may be invested in a glass of wine or a pair of boots – the icons which potentially stand for 'tradition' are always present.

### Playing on Traditional Women/Traditional Women at Play

Notions of traditional femininity play a fertile role in the imaginations of many men and women (who are often labelled sexist), but women's connections with these identities are rather tenuous. There are women who, at times, interpret some of their own (and others') experiences and activities in terms of traditional models and moralities. However, such interpretations do not imply that women conform to, or live by, these moralities or models. Moreover, whilst women do, on occasion perform in accordance to traditional models of femininity, this does not always signify that they are traditional women. My research indicated that notions of traditional femininity are used as reference points for the classification of women in bullfighting. Similarly, I found that recognisable models of femininity are woven into the strategies of women who play, or aspire to, active roles in bullfighting.

Whether or not one should conform to (or enact) traditional models is an issue which invariably becomes bound up with a range of other factors. For instance, the financial cost of buying appropriate festive, traditional clothing must be weighed up. During my fieldwork the question of whether a woman should accompany her husband or fiancé to the bullfight provoked varied responses: some men asserted that they would never consider going to the bullfight with their wives; others sometimes sat with their wives and daughters during the season of feria bullfights and on other occasions sat with their friends. For one family the question of where and with whom one should sit depended mainly on the extent of one's interest in the particular bullfighters of the day. One informant pointed out that it was not worth paying double the price to sit with her husband to see his favourite bullfighter when she would be better off saving the money for a good seat when her own favourite was performing. In contrast another informant was confronted with a dilemma when it came to buying tickets for the bullfight; he was a very dedicated television aficionado and would dearly have loved to attend the live performances of the feria, nevertheless he felt that if he bought himself tickets he would also be obliged to invite and pay for his fiancée to accompany him. This man, who was in late middle-age and with relatively little money, was most frustrated by the irony of his situation – the moral obligation he felt towards his fiancée meant that were he to attend he would have to buy cheap seats in an inferior location. The idea that women should accompany their husbands to bullfights is again reinforced by photographic reports: from the 1970s to the 1990s the audience photographs of named bullfighting celebrities 'and his wife' have been part of the visual construction of bullfights.

## Wives, Mothers and Lovers

At the beginning of this chapter I introduced the dominant models of femininity that are represented in traditional bullfighting discourse. These categories are not mutually exclusive – both the good wife and the seductress may be 'beautiful spectators', yet the latter only superficially fulfils this role since she inevitably reveals her individualistic appetite and a selfishness that endangers the bullfighter. The significance of these models lies in the way they are frequently referenced in media discourses and aficionado conversation. During my fieldwork I followed three narratives which I shall discuss below. One concerns contemporary performers, the remaining two are historical cases which were continually evoked in the media and discourses of my informants.

## Manolete: suffering mother, dangerous lover

The bullfighter *Manolete* died after being wounded whilst performing in Linares, in the Jaén Province (Andalusia) in August 1947. Accounts of his last hours stress the close relationship between the bullfighter and his mother. It is frequently reiterated that whilst there was a lament amongst Manolete's last words that his mother should be obliged to suffer his death, he did not once mention the name of his supposed fiancée, the actress Lupe Sino.

Manolete's mother, Angustias Sánchez has become a key figure in the bullfighting history of Córdoba – she is usually constructed as a symbol of feminine suffering. Her husbands who were both bullfighters, left her a widow twice over; one like Manolete was killed by a bull. Her status as the only woman who possesses a permanent place in Córdoba's bullfight exhibitions and publications is granted through her relationship to male bullfighters. Moreover, as in Mira's account, her 'life of suffering' is constructed in relation to these three performers:

> Her name, Angustias, is exactly what matches the reality of her anguished life – few women have suffered more than Doña Angustias. She was the wife of two *toreros* and the mother of one and is of an exceptional category of humanity who lived what it is to suffer being in this situation. (1984:24)

Accounts of his life and death repeatedly emphasise Manolete's strong and nurturing relationship with his mother. In interview men who worked closely with Manolete characterise his relationship with Lupe Sino as negative and problematic (see Mira 1984). It has been suggested that Manolete's death was caused when he sought refuge from a rough patch in the relationship by turning to alcohol. Some of my informants proposed that Manolete had been drunk on the day of his death. Others even suggested that he had become addicted to cocaine whilst with Lupe Sino in Mexico. It is not surprising that such theories do not surface in the respectful tributes to Manolete as triumphant hero which dominate the literature about him. I find it significant that there have been attempts to attribute Manolete's death to his relationship with Lupe Sino insofar as a similar scenario has been constructed concerning the death in 1984 of another bullfighter, *Paquirri* (see below).

In the written history of Manolete, mother and lover are set up in opposition to one another. They did not socialise in the same circles and Doña Angustias is said to have been displeased by her son's choice. Whilst the mother is always described as supportive and stabilising, Lupe Sino is portrayed as destructive and dangerous. Her unsettling influence on the emotional life of the bullfighter is said to have put him in mortal danger. Nevertheless, although there are elements of the seductress model which contribute to the representation of Lupe Sino, she does not fit the stereotype. In fact, the other side of the debate about the role of Lupe Sino represents her as an unfortunate 'hanger-on' of whom Manolete made use but with whom he was never in love. The existence of an 'unknown' local, a 'traditional Cordoban beauty' who Manolete 'should have married' has even been put forward as an alternative to Lupe Sino. Both representations of the actress assert that there was something wrong about Lupe Sino: she did not manifest traditional morality nor was she an appropriate fiancée for a bullfighter. In contrast,

Angustias Sánchez is constructed as the ideal type of woman to be the wife or mother of a bullfighter.[8] In Córdoba, her semi-religious life of suffering and her self-sacrifice for those men around her who were bullfighters gives her a special place in the bullfighting world. This is indicated by the fact that the annual memorial for the death of her son which is published in the local newspaper every year on 29 August is also dedicated to his mother.

Informants who had known Manolete's family maintained this image of Angustias Sánchez; and they did so by contrasting her to Lupe Sino. I was repeatedly told that Manolete's mother was central to my research since she is an extremely important figure in the bullfighting world. Her importance stems from her relationships with the key male figure in Cordoban bullfighting history and the kin-based continuity acknowledged by other bullfighter descendants. Most informants characterised the life of the mother of a bullfighter as one of suffering. However, when I spoke to some of the mothers of bullfighters in Córdoba I received an interesting variety of responses.

One mother told me that she had always been against her son's ambition to be a bullfighter and could not bear to watch his performances live (although she viewed some on video). Her own association with bullfighting grew from her son's involvement – she would never have considered herself an aficionada. She felt proud of her son's achievements and in that way shared his happiness, but she would prefer him to give up such a career.

Some informants suggested that the extent of a woman's suffering depends on the depth of her afición: one woman, a devoted aficionada, said that in her personal experience if one has afición, the emotional strength of the performance will elevate one's experience of the performance above the sensation of maternal worry. Afición enables one to become absorbed in the beauty and art of the bullfight. Another aficionada, the mother of a novillero bullfighter enthusiastically promoted her son and keenly awaited his performances. She explained that risk was simply part of the career of a bullfighter. She dearly loved the bullfight and would be delighted if her son could become a leading performer one day. I talked with an aficionada who was keen for her teenage son to be a bullfighter and therefore actively encouraged him to train and experiment at country festivals. In this case parental stereotypes were reversed: the father, as enthusiastic an aficionado as his wife, was much more cautious; he did not want the bullfighter's dangerous and problematic career for his son. His wife joked playfully about her deviation from the traditional maternal standpoint.

## Paquirri and Pantoja: Perfect wife or adulterous flirt?

The romance between bullfighter Paquirri and his second wife, Isabel Pantoja, a Tonderillera (a singer of traditional Spanish song) received much media attention – the Torero–Tonderillera marriage is often considered an ideal match. As icons of traditional masculinity and femininity they form the dyad which is central to constructions of social order in bullfighting discourses.

Paquirri died after being wounded by a bull in Pozoblanco in the Córdoba province in 1984. Informants told me that in the weeks which followed his death, Pantoja became the 'national widow.' She was already a national media figure, and as the idea of the 'national' loss of a hero was invested in her media image an identity was created which was apparently compatible with her own performance of grief. Paquirri's death was recorded on video and was followed by the publication of several books as well as numerous commemorative magazine articles and supplements. Much of this literature focused on Pantoja, working her grief into a romantic frame of tragedy and suffering. In one Cordoban publication a whole set of articles was dedicated to Isabel Pantoja. The author of one contribution told me he had stopped his car to write the piece on hearing the news of the torero's death over the car radio. Several of my informants had written to Pantoja personally to express their condolences (see Toscano 1984). It is not unusual that the death of a bullfighter should result in the showering of public attention on his family. For example, in 1992 when a banderillero was killed in the bullring, a national fund was set up and a stream of donations, administered by *Aplausos* magazine was channelled towards the economic support of his wife and family.

Some media laments of Paquirri's death represent the Paquirri–Pantoja relationship as the 'perfect marriage' made between two 'traditional, sincere and honest people.' Gargilla (1989) predicts that their future would have been equally perfect. Nevertheless, in the ensuing years the narrative has become more complex, and in particular another curious strand of speculation over the cause of Paquirri's death has developed. Several men and women informants told me that Pantoja's position as the 'national widow' was rather ironic since she had actually been instrumental in her husband's death. One informant suggested that Paquirri had been drinking heavily before his last performance because his marriage was on the rocks and his wife was having numerous affairs. Other accusations have been more subtle, but the same theme persists: Pantoja and Paquirri were having marital difficulties and the bullfighter was unable to concentrate on his performance. Even explanations which emphasise that the couple were deeply in love tend to blame Pantoja for her husband's death. For example, ex-bullfighter Miguel Dominguín commented that:

> Some days before Paquirri died we were watching a programme down here and I noticed how he was watching his wife sing until 1 a.m. in the morning. I thought: it's not important because he's not drinking or anything and he's a strong man who trains a lot; but he's in love with his wife – something which seems fantastic – but one pays for it. (Zumbiehl 1987)

During my fieldwork the media controversy lived on. In 1990 Paquirri's brother accused Isabel Pantoja of arguing with Paquirri the night before his death, and refusing to speak with him when he attempted to telephone her just before his fatal performance the next day. Further speculations culminated in 1993 in a much publicised appearance of Paquirri's father on a TV 'real-life' show. He was wired to a 'lie detector' machine and subjected to a test (which was administered by a German doctor) about the couple's relationship. Some informants were glued to their screens. Those with whom I viewed were sufficiently interested to zap between channels to catch some minor details. At any rate, the results were reported in the press the following day. The outcome was not decisive and the alleged marital dispute has never been 'proven.' Nevertheless, the controversies have shaken Pantoja's status as national widow for some viewers. Pantoja has been a favourite media chameleon, and as a media woman she has been moulded to symbolise the traditional femininities of both seductress and faithful wife. Making decisions about media women such as Pantoja is a subjective enterprise. In my experience the debate is held over cups of coffee and around the television. The classifications which one places on her seem to depend upon which narrative one wants to attach to her at the time: she may simultaneously stand for the duality in 'every woman' that some informants spoke of, or, she may be seen less symbolically as a famous widow about whom the media tell stories.

## Does Sex Destroy a Bullfighter's Career?

Some bullfighters and aficionados uphold the argument that women and bullfighting can be a deadly combination. The deaths of Manolete and Paquirri were connected to their relationships with women; and Marvin (1988) notes that Paquirri was once criticised for 'saving himself for Pantoja' and not giving his all to the performance. The demise of leading bullfighter *Espartaco* was likewise attributed to his marriage in 1991; and both media and aficionado discourse claimed that he took still fewer risks after the birth of his first child. The idea that bullfighters should avoid sexual intercourse before performing or even during the whole of the bullfighting season is quite widespread. Some believe that sexual intercourse or simply contact with women may sap the strength of the performer (Marvin 1988: 153–4). Ex-bullfighter Miguel Dominguín explains the problem as not simply of sexual intercourse, but of falling in love, claiming every scar on his body was won in 'the name of a woman' with whom he believed himself to be in love and for whom he had lost concentration whilst in the arena (see Zumbiehl 1989).

Whilst the sex lives of bullfighters are usually represented as having a negative affect on their performances, the 'right woman' may be treated as a positive influence. The case of Rocío Jurado and Ortega Cano shows how this idea can be developed in aficionado and media discourse. Rocío Jurado, like Isabel Pantoja, is a Tonderillera or *Coplista*. The issue of the Tonderillera–Torero association was raised by Rocío in a 1975 interview: 'I have never allowed myself to become emotionally involved with a bullfighter – isn't that strange for a singer like me? – I've always seen the torero as a dangerous man for a woman.' She characterised the life of a bullfighter's wife as a very sad existence, and the torero as not her type of man (*El Ruedo*, 1975). Almost twenty years later, when she was in the process of divorcing her first husband Rocío Jurado's happy romance with a leading torero became news. Far from being characterised by suffering, Rocío's face is described as 'evidencing enormous happiness' as she watches Cano's performance (*Pronto*, 1993). The bullfight press attributed Ortega Cano's success to his flourishing personal life and Rocío was frequently photographed in the audience at his performances. This media romance was constructed as a serious love affair which lent strength to other aspects of both performers' lives; Rocío Jurado's career was also at a high point – in

1993 she starred in a feature film and brought out a new record. The question of how Ortega Cano's career was affected by his being in love was addressed in detail by the media. In 1993 the television show *Queremos Saber* (We Want to Know) took up the issue and interviewed the couple. Many of my informants certainly did 'want to know' so did I! – but this eagerness must be qualified by the number of viewers who dismissed the programme as rubbish. The interview, which included footage from the performances of both Ortega and Rocío, to my mind represented a balanced and healthy romance which had led to emotional fulfilment and professional achievement. Evidence was presented to publicly deny that their relationship had ever had any negative affect on Cano's performances. Bullfighting journalists supported this view; for instance, Manuel Moles wrote that 'everyone thought that between his romance with Rocío and his age, Ortega was finished, but in fact he has continued to perform as well if not better than ever' (*El Ruedo*, 15 January 1993). Similarly, in a press interview, Cano stated that 'love helps and strengthens a man of my age . . . the fact that I am in love . . . has not affected my work, on the contrary, it has strengthened me' (*Diario 16*, 3 August 1993).[9] Such commentaries represent tradition as a nourishing force.

## Traditional Tales and their Transient Hosts

The relationship between traditional narratives of gender role segregation that specifically refer to bullfighting culture, individual subjectivities and the experiences of particular women in bullfighting is complex and uneven. The so-called traditional themes of feminine spectator, seductress, and the 'woman who prays', considered alongside the 'perfect traditional couple', may be usefully regarded as a cultural resource which is on tap for classifying and thus making meaningful certain experiences and activities. This however does not mean that social behaviour, life and experience is conveniently patterned and ordered in terms of these different masculine and feminine types. Neither do they represent a dominant discourse on, or form of, women's oppression. Rather these identities are constantly set up anew as reference points; they are used to explore and express identities and difference and to locate self and other in particular visions of social reality. In this sense, narratives of tradition may be used parasitically to feed off the women who (sometimes unwillingly) become their hosts.

Representations of traditional gender are part of the contemporary social and cultural landscape of Andalusia in the 1990s. As I have described in Chapter 1, as a cultural resource they are used in a variety of different ways. For example, representations of traditional moralities may be woven into gossip strategies and as such they can be used to critique, or comment upon behaviour. Alternatively, they may be set up in opposition to other models of masculinity and femininity so as to be critiqued themselves. Models of traditional femininity are often used to argue that women should not perform as bullfighters. As such they are employed to symbolise a certain version of social order that is often equated with the bullfighting world. However, they should not be taken as representations of women's activity and experience of bullfighting. In the next chapter I develop this theme further to explore some of the roles women play in the production and practices of bullfighting culture.

# Notes

1. This is different from the claim that she represents feminine moral integrity which is made by Pink and Sanders (1996), and by Pitt-Rivers (1963).

2. See, for example, Conrad's *Death of a Matador* (1952); *Sangre y Arena* (Blasco Ibañez 1991), from which a theatre production and three film versions have been produced; and *La mujer, el torero y el toro* (Insúa 1971).

3. Mitchell's maja is not prominent in Cordoban bullfighting history. My informants knew the word for its contemporary meaning: in the words of one woman, 'a maja is a girl who is a good person, she doesn't have to be really pretty, but is attractive because she is overall a good person.' I was told the term is not used in Córdoba, but is from Madrid and further north. Some Valencians frequently described a person as *muy maja* to say she is a 'good person.'

4. The controversy developed partially owing to the British censor's decision to cut the more sexually explicit shots from the original version that was screened in Spain.

5. The choice of this era for analysis was a deliberate design to encompass a historical period during which there has been accelerated social change, and in which the position of women has altered enormously. Although the clothing of photographic subjects has changed, the iconography has remained relatively constant.

6. Whilst I was learning bullfighting photography I followed the same format. It occurred to me less frequently to photograph male friends in the audience, although I did come away with several photographs of women with their eyes keenly set on the action.

7. In the case of this *becerrada* the women who (for example) participate in the bawdy female crowd take part for a range of different personal motives. Their behaviour, rather than reflecting or inverting their everyday lives or experiences, should be interpreted as their representations of tradition. In this sense, 'festive behaviour' does not represent a statement about everyday life. Rather it may be regarded as a collectivity of subjective interpretations of tradition and a performance of those notions of tradition. Such performances of tradition may not be intended to advocate a traditional way of life, but rather to enjoy a traditional activity.

8. Wives of bullfighters are often expected to become the mothers of bullfighters since it is considered usual that the sons of bullfighters should wish to follow their father's career.

9. The Jurado–Cano romance stimulated a whole series of articles about the tonderillera–torero relationship. In one article about the history of the 'traditional couple' the journalist, Marcelo González, listed twenty-seven such couples.

# Active Aficionadas: A Gendered Lens on a Photographic Ritual

## Women in Bullfighting or Bullfighting in Women?

In Córdoba I sought out women who had some presence in bullfighting. I was intrigued to learn of their experiences of being a torero, ganadera (breeder), *apoderada* (manager), *periodista* (journalist), peña member, mother or wife. Each woman constructed, challenged or restated traditional and other femininities in her own personal style.

The bullfighting world is frequently represented as a domain inhabited by men to whom the lives of women are relative and marginal. Women who reach the headlines or who are discussed in *aficionado* discourse tend to be those who are exceptional and in the public gaze – most commonly those who succeed as bullfighters. As for sport 'most people know about exceptional sports women . . . but . . . little is known about the various types of women who participate who are involved in sports, and the values that they bring to them' (Hargreaves 1994: 1). Active aficionadas undoubtedly have some impact on how values are articulated in bullfighting circles. In this chapter I shall explore some of the strategies by which women operate in bullfighting, and how different women incorporate bullfighting's apparently masculine discourse into their feminine identities. Finally I will focus on a more detailed example of women as the producers of bullfighting photography.

Performing as a bullfighter perhaps may appear to be the most controversial role that a woman may play in the bullfighting world and it can represent a very public statement about gender. A variety of reactions will always greet any woman involved in bullfighting. The grounds upon which women are accepted or rejected are rearticulated in each situation. Thus women who operate in bullfighting culture often navigate its networks and gossips by playing off different representations of their own feminine identities against the femininities referred to by traditional discourses. As my project progressed I sometimes perceived myself as a subject of this research: a woman in a world of bullfighting. At times I attempted to mimic feminine models, hoping to be accepted; often my involvement entailed opting to act the role of writer and photographer. Other roles were less comfortable, in particular, the possibility that I should begin a programme of training at the bullfighting school! It seemed that a 'logical' conclusion of learning about bullfighting is the practical application of that knowledge. For instance, this may occur at a country fiesta where an opportunity to attempt a cape pass with a young cow could arise. I was confident that were I to learn the passes I would never perform them: I had no illusions about becoming a bullfighter, and would have been ridiculed had I tried. I watched others train, trying to kindle a sense of inspiration for that 'moment of truth' – the confrontation with a live animal – but I knew I would never step out, cape in hand, to face even the smallest cow. I declined offers of tutoring – there were plenty of young hopefuls at the bullfighting school and too few teachers to go around as it was!

## Anthropologist as Aficionada

In Córdoba, when my interest in bullfighting became well known, some male informants began to refer to me as an aficionada. My rare combination of 'Englishness' and afición was a frequent source of delight that for some implied a victory over the anti-bullfighting movement. It also endowed me with a useful novelty value. Initially it puzzled me that my minimal knowledge of bullfighting was sufficient for me to be referred to as an aficionada. However, in practice, the term is used to express a variety of degrees of understanding, knowledge and interest in bullfighting; its meaning is contextual, sometimes qualified by use of the term *verdadera aficionada* (true aficionada). My English afición was deemed to be exceptional, there are other explanations for the existence of Spanish aficionadas.

## Becoming an Aficionada: in the veins or in the air?

Most women who called themselves aficionadas explained that they developed their afición in childhood. Those from families involved in the business or practice of bullfighting usually attributed their afición to family socialisation – attending bullfights, country festivals, visiting ganaderías. Most possessed extensive knowledge of bullfighting in addition to practical experience. Other women credited their afición to male relatives whom they accompanied to the bullfight when they were children. One woman whose ambition was to be a critic regularly visited the bullring with her father, a taurine vet. Others, uninterested until marriage said they had 'caught' their husband's afición. By contrast, men are thought to 'inherit' afición: it is in their blood.

## Situating Afición in Women's Narratives

It is useful to consider the viewing practices of aficionadas in terms of personal and family lifestyle and consumption patterns. These practices apply to both live and televised bullfights, the latter will be discussed in detail in Chapter 8. As I described in the previous chapter, amongst my informants a few women attended live performances alone, others went as a family outing, and some went with their peer group or with a bullfighting club. Most of the women I spoke with watched televised bullfights, and some middle-aged women called themselves 'television aficionadas' – rather than participating in the social life or performance of the bullfight they followed televised and written reports.

Many women attend bullfighting peñas and their accompanying social events. Whereas married women often participate on the strength of their husband's membership, younger women lead a social life in the youth peñas that is characterised by peer-group equality whilst also often patronised by paternal support. Some teenage girls sign up at the bullfighting school, not out of an aspiration to be a bullfighter, but as an assertion that to understand truly the bullfight they must have practical knowledge of technique. Students attend courses, seminars and conferences to study the theory, history and philosophy of bullfighting.

I discovered that other women's social lives were devoted to events and friendships connected with the bullfighting world. The wife of an ex-bullfighter radio and television bullfight journalist, found that her life was dominated by bullfighting events either as leisure or in connection with her husband's work. She said this was 'ideal', she had grown up in an aficionado family, adored bullfighting, and was delighted by the recent marriage of her daughter to a ganadero.

## How do Women Channel their Afición?

Women express and enact their interest in bullfighting in diverse ways that meet with various degrees of approval. Some informants told me the most proper way for an aficionada to be involved in a bullfighting career is to marry a bullfighter; her role is to provide him with the necessary support and understanding. The ex-bullfighter's wife whom I interviewed appeared to perform a similar role. When I met her she was about to leave her flat to collect one of her husband's colleagues who was arriving at the train station. They would then both go on to join her husband and other colleagues for a business lunch. In this respect her involvement directly supported her husband's salaried work. Other informants suggested that as a manager or sponsor a woman may prove her afición by investing her economic resources in the supportive promotion of a male performer – this particular role was one initiated by another woman I met during my fieldwork.

One woman, a ganadera, channeled her interest in bullfighting into the management of her ganadería and the taking on of a leading role in professional associations. She argued that although women do not have a physically suitable build to perform, they can and should pursue other careers in bullfighting. However, women who own ganaderías are positioned differently from those who are involved through the peñas. Informants identified the ganadera's position as a traditional feminine role, but they assumed that most ganaderas hired men to manage their ganaderías. An active ganadera is empowered in ways most aficionadas are not. She has a direct claim to a place in the bullfighting world, and she possesses the social status and financial backing to move easily in its élite circles.

Nevertheless, the absence of the formal influence of women in the peñas should not be interpreted as absolute disempowerment. Women's power is articulated in social networks which join bullfight aficionado families and individuals. For example, the wife of one ex-bullfighter put her network of contacts (*enchufes*) into motion to secure a manager for her nephew, a would-be bullfighter. When I carried out a series of interviews with women relatives of bullfighters I found that I was passed along the friendship and kinship networks of women. Through this I learnt how these women's connections form a crucial part of the complex webs of social relationships, political power and patronage by which the bullfighting world is organised.

Moreover, in the 1990s an increasing number of women are becoming bullfighting professionals. Amongst my informants young women wove their interest in bullfighting into their professional development by training in photography, journalism, and veterinary science with the stated intention of applying these skills to a career in bullfighting.

## Women and the Peñas

Most of my informants agreed that the peñas[1] are attended by 'aficionados and their families'. Meetings are normally held in bars where the peñas are permanently based. Members organise a variety of fund-raising activities (such as lotteries, annual dinners), their profits subsidise spring and autumn bull-festivals in the countryside, winter lectures, round table discussions, video and film screenings, and subsidised coach trips to see the club's bullfighter perform in other cities.[2] Peñas present annual trophies for the May feria bullfights, and some use their funds to support young aspiring bullfighters by arranging promotional performances. The biggest clubs are amongst the eighty or so local organisations which construct the portable decorative bars *(casetas)* during the May feria, thus they can be seen as standing for the institutions of traditional life.

In Córdoba there are approximately fifty peñas of varying size and longevity. Their membership ranges from three people to over seventy. I visited many peñas and became more involved with four. One was held on private premises, comprised close friends and family, and met on an informal basis; another was exclusively male with six regular members, was held in a traditional bar and dedicated to the bullfighter Manolete; the third club, one of the largest, was of mixed sex and age and dedicated to Finito de Córdoba; the fourth was the university bullfighting club, which was led by two male students, had a mixed-sex membership, and published a successful intellectual bullfighting journal. I also participated in activities organised by a number of other peñas.[3]

## Women and Membership of the Peñas

Not all men who attend peñas are members. Several of those with whom I spoke refused to commit themselves to a particular club. They explained that they preferred to have good relations with all the clubs rather than being obliged to deal with the petty quarrels

**Figure 11:** During my excursion around Córdoba with Cristina Sánchez and her hosts photographing was a part of the occasion. I photographed Cristina with the members of a Cordoban *peña* in the bar where they usually met. In this case a group of men had met for a pre-lunch drink. *Peñas* are an important part of the social life of bullfighting and it was considered important that Cristina should experience this aspect of the bullfighting world of the city.

© Sarah Pink

and organisational problems of just one. In general, I found that women and men tended to negotiate their status in the clubs differently. I received mixed responses to my initial questions about women's membership of peñas. Some informants said women only attended 'events', others told me that peñas had male and female members. However, some peñas did appear to be exclusively male. I found that many informants were often uncertain of the status of women in the peñas. In general, it seems that in Córdoba, adult women often participate in, but are not listed as, members of bullfighting clubs. I discovered that whilst women's peñas existed elsewhere in Spain none were active in Córdoba between 1992 and 1994. In comparison, in the youth sections of peñas, both sexes possess formal membership and assume leadership and organisational roles. One man explained that women's membership was not a necessity because women attended with their husbands. Others told me that women had no personal interest and simply accompanied their male relatives. It is true that sometimes women do enact this role. For example, when I attended a lecture in Córdoba's élite bullfighting club there were three women in late middle-age in the audience. One woman left when the talk ended, of the two who remained for the drinks reception one told me that as the sister of the speaker she had attended in order to support her brother, and her friend had accompanied her so that she shouldn't have to go alone.

The exclusively male peña (which I refer to above) held weekly meetings to 'chat' and deal with administration and organisation. Women were not privy to these sessions but attended their occasional lectures and fiestas. The large club was 'family orientated' and, for some, weekly meetings centered on a lecture series which was organised by the youth section. Some participation patterns appeared to be gendered. Men only tended to enter the lecture if they were particularly interested in the theme or speaker. Families usually separated on arrival – men would congregate around the bar whilst their wives, mothers and children immediately occupied the seats arranged for the lecture. This pattern was not absolutely rigid: some women debated with men at the bar, and men often joined in conversations at the tables. However, I perceived general differences in gender roles to be apparent. In this peña 'senior' activities were controlled by a core of older men, women did not participate formally in organisation or decision making, although some did feel free to express opinions. Informants reported that the same was true for other peñas. One young woman complained bitterly about a situation where 'serious' matters (official business, decision making and administration) were closely guarded by senior men. In this large family peña, she said, these leaders took women's subscriptions and gave them Christmas lottery tickets to sell, but when important policy issues or debates arose women members were excluded. Nevertheless, in the 1990s women's presence is growing in bullfighting peñas. In youth sections teenage girls participate in and have responsibility for, activities on an equal footing with their male contemporaries – the president of one youth division was an efficient teenage girl. However, older women are often situated with reference to a more traditional notion of femininity. Few women attend peña events alone; my attendance at the exclusively male bullfighting club was facilitated by a friend who was the treasurer of the club. One sunny winter morning I arrived alone at the coach stop to go on a day-trip to see the family club's bullfighter perform. When I paid the club's president for my ticket he pointed to the far end of the coach. 'The other girls are all sitting down there on the back seat,' he said, suggesting that I join them. Although I was at least ten years older than the other girls, to his mind a young single woman had no place in the senior section.

### Bullfighting, Youth and the Peñas

Teenage aficionadas do not cede control to their male contemporaries.[4] Yet their power does not extend outside the 'youth' sphere. My teenage informants planned to take leading roles as adult women but these aspirations are not yet realised.

Some informants dealt with teenage girls' achievements by classifying them as more mature, responsible and organised than boys of their own age. They expected girls to be more interested in administrative activities and boys to dedicate their efforts to training to bullfight. These notions of gender may be reinforced when girls and boys enact certain roles. For instance, in Córdoba two teenage girls managed a series of promotional bullfights; whilst the boys tended to envisage themselves as bullfighters and thus devoted their energy to preparing themselves rather than to promoting the careers of their contemporaries. The organisers of these events were around fifteen years old, members of youth bullfighting clubs and had strong family contacts in bullfighting. The role they carved for themselves was prominent but did not involve their stepping into a masculine performing role. Instead, they performed fund-raising and administrative roles which, as I have suggested above, are more often classified as appropriate feminine activities. Their project was legitimised and backed by male members of the bullfighting community, the girls were from 'good' families and considered trustworthy. Moreover, in organising promotional event, they did not trespass upon the realm of serious bullfighting. Their work was complementary to that of male teenagers, voluntary, and represented no real challenge to traditional discourses, or at least it could easily be made safe within the boundaries of these discourses. Simultaneously, the young women were advancing their own careers in another domain: they were hoping to improve their CVs.

## Traditional Icons and Gendered Knowledge

The interface between photography, bullfighting and identity is a complex and fascinating aspect of bullfighting culture (see Pink 1996b, 1997a). An exploration of how women's aficionada identities are made meaningful through photography is indicative not only of perceptions of women in bullfighting, but of how notions of tradition, ritual and gender are articulated and visualised in contemporary Andalusia.

Bullfighting photography tends to be used 'honorifically': formal portraiture and shots of 'triumphal moments' and 'great performances' endow status upon the bullfighter.[5] Since the nineteenth-century inception of photography in bullfighting culture, technological innovation has facilitated images of a higher quality but the basic iconography has not changed. The maintenance of conventions in bullfighting photography represents a curious example of how the visual imagery of traditional discourse, referred to in the previous chapter, coexists with, and in this case supports, activities which may be considered to contradict traditional gender configurations. Women photographers produce bullfighting images that repeat the gendered iconography of conventional visual compositions whilst overtly voicing and enacting disagreement with the idea that women should be supportive beautiful spectators and men triumphant heroes. When browsing through the portfolios of women amateur photographers and reflecting on my own imitations of bullfight photography, I encountered series after series of images of men performing and women spectating. In part I measured my own understanding of the bullfight through my ability to produce photographs of it that my informants approved of. In doing so I was learning to watch the bullfight in a particular way and I was being encouraged to adopt a certain perspective. As women learn to be aficionadas their subjectivities become interwoven with these visual discourses which can be interpreted as the imposition of a 'masculine gaze' on the performance. However it is clear that ways of understanding a performance do not lead to ways of constructing social order. The distance between the gendered iconography represented in photographs as cultural products and the gendered identities and polemics expressed by their producers as 'what I believe in' indicates how these photographic constructions of ritual may be used to represent a discourse that is appreciated but not lived. Thus, it appears to be the case that photographic renderings of bullfights comprise visual constructions of tradition in which tradition is treated as a commodity rather than a justification for the social order.

Visual histories of Cordoban bullfighting celebrate local masculine triumph; its iconography is of individualistic masculine achievement. Those excluded from these visual histories are not seen to have contributed to the glorious history of bullfighting in Córdoba. Photographs of bullfighting's failures do not pertain to the local history of heroes. Some find their place of privilege on the wall of their protagonist's home, but their wider historical value is doubtful. Through these displays bullfight photography is used to represent a historical tradition. I shall explore below how women photographers and their work are interpreted in bullfighting circles – both the representations made by the person looking through the lens and the discourses produced by those who gaze at her will be of interest.

## Long Lenses and Big Arenas

Córdoba's feria bullfights which are held in May are meticulously documented in the local press and television. After feria in 1993 I left Spain for a few days, on my return my partner greeted me at the station with the news that I had 'been on television': a three-second shot of me taking a photo during a feria bullfight had been broadcast on the regional television news. In this rather unexceptional piece of footage I had been performing the feminine role of image producer and spectator, some viewers probably assumed that I was taking a holiday snap of a bullfighter (maybe I was – see Pink 1996c). In this media imagery the role of 'woman as spectator as photographer' was compatible with a representation of a traditional ritual. Moreover, those viewers who knew I was an anthropologist would have had no trouble reconciling my presence with the bullfight – Spanish 'traditions' are studied by Spanish and foreign academics alike. However, specific feminine identities are not constructed solely in connection with the practice of photographing. Rather, a woman may be classified by the type of photographs she produces. I was enacting the role of amateur photographer (see below). Firstly, I shall consider professional and publishable work.

Official photography is built into the structure of the performance, and professional photographers are amongst the actors. Even before they share the arena with the bull the bullfighters encounter the photographers who represent news agencies and papers. Throughout the bullfight they stand, leaning forward, in a special ringside location, their long powerful zoom lenses pointed towards the action. The reports usually include photographs of: the *paseillo* (entrance to the ring); the bullfighter performing cape passes; a picador properly spearing the bull; a banderillero skilfully placing the banderillas; the bullfighter dedicating his bull to the audience, challenging the bull and the final stages of his *muleta* (red cape) passes; the ultimate successful kill; the bullfighter standing victorious over the dead bull and triumphant with arms extended upwards displaying his trophies (ears or tails); the super-triumphal bullfighter carried out of the arena on the shoulders of the crowd. In addition, one often sees images of the audience, bulls, of people in danger, and of human death. Bullfighting imagery weaves narratives of success, triumph or tragedy; not of failure – the dead bullfighter becomes a tragic hero.[6] Performers and photographers respond to conventions: bullfighters assume poses or perform actions to express a triumphant self to their audience, and such moments create photographic opportunities. Photographers are expected to be ready to record exceptional performances and to capture those 'special moments' which may occur on the periphery of the arena. It is in this respect that some aficionados suggest that specialist photographers exhibit greater bullfighting spirit than the toreros – it is they who capture more fully the beauty of the event (for example, de Córdoba 1990: 11).

In Córdoba, photographers of the bullfight are honoured; one family in particular has been associated with bullfighting photography for several generations and their collective work is commemorated in a book (see Ladis 1991). Photographs are frequently taken to indicate their creator's understanding of the bullfight. Successful performance photography requires an in-depth knowledge of the nature of performance, technique, bulls, the styles of particular bullfighters and the current state of affairs in the bullfighting world. In the words of the critic José Luis de Córdoba, 'Some people think that an indispensable condition for being a good taurine photographer is to have been a bullfighter, or at least to be a practical aficionado' (1990: 11). Bullfighting photographers autograph their photographs with bold clear signatures that form part of the aesthetic affect of the photograph. It is these signatures which identify the photographer as author and artist. Thus a photographer's work may be interpreted as an expression of his/her own relationship to, and subjective understanding of, the bullfight. The assertion that only a range of knowledge which almost equals that of the bullfighter is sufficient to enable one to photograph a performance defines both the bullfighter and the photographer as artists.

Feiner (1995: 356–7) stresses the obstacles confronted by women bullfighting photographers. In particular, she quotes the war photographer Christine Spengler who found that men would not allow her to enter places 'unsuitable for women' such as the *callejon* of the arena, or the car in which the matador and his cuadrilla travel. Nevertheless, in the 1980s and 1990s an increasing number of women have become bullfighting photographers. In Córdoba, one woman, Olga, stands amongst her male colleagues at the ringside. She is married to a banderillero and is involved in bullfighting professionally and socially. For aficionados Olga is primarily a photographer of the bullfight, yet she works on many local photojournalistic assignments, as do many men otherwise known as 'bullfight photographers'. It seems that, on this local stage, women photographers whose work (and social contacts) exhibit adequate afición are well placed to secure bullfighting assignments. However, for aficionados, bullfighting photography is not 'just another assignment'; it demands a 'bullfighter's' sense and understanding of the performance.

### Shorter Lenses and Amateur Eyes

Some aficionados told me that they combined an interest in photography with a passion for bullfighting. Thus, according to them, their photographic practices are experienced as an expression of afición. Others, who identified their principal hobby as photography, lauded the bullfight as a fine photographic subject. In

**Figure 12:** With a good zoom lens, fast film and a reasonably good seat it is possible for a serious amateur to take acceptable photographs. I took this photograph with a Pentax camera, zoom lens, 400 ASA colour film and good light conditions, sitting about a quarter of the arena away from the action. Note the professional photographers shooting these key moments from their ringside vantage points, as Finito de Córdoba kills his bull.

© Sarah Pink

**Figure 13**: This photograph of the *picador* stage was taken under the same conditions described for Figure 12.

© Sarah Pink

Córdoba the practice of bullfighting photography appeared to be a trend amongst some educated middle-class girls in their late teens. Whilst they situated themselves primarily as aficionadas, their gender inevitably influenced other people's expectations and interpretations of the photographs they produced. Simultaneously, evaluation of the aficionado status of a photographer (as a subjective gendered observer of the bullfight) can be contingent on the composition, subject matter, artistic value and conventional conformity displayed in the images which they create. In other words, whilst the gendered identity of the photographer informs one about his/her subjectivity as an image producer; simultaneously, the photographer's image–products inform one about the integrity of his/her afición.

In my experience, keen amateurs tend to imitate professional styles. With a zoom lens, a high-speed film and a seat near the ringside most amateurs can produce photographs comparable to journalistic work (see Figures 12 and 13). Thus, it seems that the production of conventional 'publication standard' images is not the exclusive privilege of professional photographers with a ringside vantage point. However, the financial outlay required for equipment and tickets restricts the production of high-quality prints to those who can finance this expensive hobby. I believe it is important to bear in mind that the images produced by amateurs and profess-ionals have different destinations. Amateurs enter photographic competitions but they photograph mainly for personal use, they share images with friends and/or display them in bullfighting peñas. Whilst amateurs will imitate professional formats they are not under a similar pressure to produce. Some amateurs play self-assigned roles by collaborating with amateur bullfighters who are infrequently photographed until they achieve success. These photographic alliances are often contextualised by kinship connections and social networks.

I believe that the gendering of serious amateur photographic production cannot be understood in terms of a simple dichotomy between masculine and feminine activity. Some young women appear to represent the combination of a 'feminine' role with 'masculine' knowledge. Through their photography they represent an understanding of afición that some men classify as truly 'masculine'. However, they are located in the feminine domain of the audience. As I have shown in Chapter 1, such young women map out their social and geographical worlds with different boundaries to those which are drawn by others who wish to locate them in a 'women's world' distinct from the (malestream) world of bullfighting. I found that, in general, the role of woman photographer was more easily accepted amongst my informants than that of woman bullfighter. Some said that since certain types of photography have long been classified as feminine professions it was quite 'natural' for women to photograph the bullfight. Others were able to fit the woman photographer neatly into another gender dichotomy: whereas young men were expected to express their interest in bullfighting by training as bullfighters or participating in country fiestas, young women may articulate their enthusiasm through photography. Significantly, a young woman who succeeds in combining photography with an informed viewing of the bullfight, is seen to represent her understanding of the event through her photography and thus she proves her 'true' afición. Therefore she disassociates herself from a notion of femininity which portrays women as incapable of understanding the 'true' nature of bull-fighting and attracted only by the sexuality of the bullfighters and the excitement of danger.

### Snapping up the Bullfighter

By contrast, snapshot photography of the bullfight is often situated in direct opposition to the 'serious' documentation of a perform-ance. In this genre the characters of the photographic story change as the photographer's visual quest seeks social rather than bullfight experience. Neither the perfection of photographic technique nor the complete documentation of the performance (rendered imposs-ible by technological limitations) are feasible objectives. When the snapshot photographer chooses the performance as his/her subject, the resulting photograph is likely to lack both formal aesthetic appeal and detail, and the larger–than–life bullfighter of the closeup shots becomes an inappropriately small figure in the middle of a large yellow arena. The takers of snapshots have few pretensions to professionalism, they aim to produce photographs which will become meaningful in other ways. Rather than attending to the social uses of snapshot photography I want to consider briefly how these images can be made meaningful in terms of traditional dis-courses on gender.

Whilst the work of serious amateurs is said to illustrate afición, some snapshots are interpreted as representations of their producers' lack of 'true' afición. They are associated with a particular under-standing of the bullfight that is labelled feminine; in this inter-pretation the (female) spectator is transfixed by the bullfighter but has no understanding of the performance. This (feminine) gaze is thus believed to photograph the bullfighter rather than the bullfight. Such an interpretation tends to be perpetuated by certain circumstances and practicalities of the bullfight. For instance, in the absence of a zoom lens, the snapshotter's greatest photographic opportunities occur only during a performer's triumphal walk around the ringside, and before or after the bullfight when the performers will walk from their cars to the bullring or hotel. It is commonplace for crowds of fans to gather outside the hotels where a related style of bullfighting photography is practised. Some fans seek to be photographed with a bullfighter or they will ask a performer to sign a photograph which was shot before or after a previous bullfight. This is the sole chance for most teenage girls to meet bullfighters and photography is woven into the process of meeting, recording, signing and remembering these fleeting moments of limited human contact with a star. Whilst young women who practise photography under these circumstances might be true aficionadas, such activity can also be referred to another narrative by which women's photography is inspired by sexual attraction and admiration, not by afición. In this respect they are in danger of being set up in opposition to those who express understanding through their photography, in the words of one teenage amateur photographer – 'there are a lot of girls who go to the bullfight at the moment because it is fashionable and they fancy the bullfighters. What they are doing is really silly and it spoils the way people see girls like us who are real aficionadas'.

However, it is not only young women who strive to have their photograph taken alongside a bullfighter, it is also a practice of men aficionados of all ages. In some situations this forms a strategy for locating oneself in the bullfighting world, and entails the construction of a visual representation of a ego-centered bullfighting world. In the course of my fieldwork I learnt that people were expected to want to be photographed with bullfighters. When Cristina Sánchez visited Córdoba I was generously invited to spend the day with her and her hosts to take photographs of the day and to meet Cristina. During my fieldwork informants only requested to take photographs with my camera twice. On this particular occasion one of my Cordoban hosts asked to take a photograph of me sitting

**Figure 14:** This photograph of me with Cristina Sánchez was taken when an informant requested my camera to provide me with an appropriate visual image.
Photograph by an unidentified informant.

**Figure 15:** Cristina Sánchez signing a copy of *The Bullfighter's Braid* that had been reproduced as the back cover of a bullfighting journal *Boletín de Loterías y Toros.*
© Sarah Pink

beside Cristina outside the bar where she was being interviewed by
a local journalist. I later developed this photograph that I was meant
to have wanted (see Figure 14). During her visit Cristina was given
the same official photographic treatment as that afforded to other
bullfighters. In the evening she gave a short lecture which was
followed by questions from the audience. Cameras flashed and
clicked throughout the meeting but it was after the speeches that
the most intense photographic activity began. I was asked to
photograph groups of aficionados/aficionadas with Cristina. Some
handed me their own cameras for the task, others with whom I was
in frequent contact asked me to supply copies. Some clasped signed
photos to their chests, others produced a well-practised grin.
Interestingly, on this occasion, the woman bullfighter was being
incorporated into the traditional iconography of the bullfight, yet
she was cast in a masculine role. Her performance of this social role
was praised by all the men and women participants I later spoke
with, although as one man put it, 'she was very good, but of course
the real test will be to see her perform in the arena.'

## Accessible Ascending Stars and Aspiring Artists

Photo-journalists are seldom interested in minor taurine events in
which aspiring beginners or unknown bullfighters perform. At the
early stages of a performer's career most photographs are taken by
his/her friends or family. Both men and women participate in
this photographic activity. The images (often a combination of
photographs and video footage) are produced for a dual purpose.
Firstly they are intended as a visual record of the performance that
the performer and other experts may use to scrutinise his/her style.
Second the images produced during a bullfighter's first performances
are frequently used in order to construct a memory or a record of
the early stages of a potentially triumphant career.

Some amateurs tend to disassociate their 'serious' photography
from family photography. One young woman stressed that whilst
she was prepared to photograph her family when they engaged in
bullfighting activities, her photography was too serious for 'trivial'
family snaps. In her opinion, her family photographs are intended
to represent her family in relation to the bullfight. Other families
similarly express their aficionado identities through their family's
bullfighting photography. For example, shots of the older children
or parents performing with young bulls often form part of family
collections. The childhood images of aficionado families frequently

include shots of young children attempting cape passes with the family dog or cat, or with their siblings. These are deemed to be representations of normal young afición; established bullfighters often cite their first bullfighting experiences as being childhood games played with domestic pets. Whilst many non-aficionado men and women informants also remembered playing at bulls and bullfighters with their siblings, the images of those who become bullfighters are lent particular significance as the celebrity's first signs of afición.

Photography (and video footage) is also produced at promotional bullfights. Such images are often used as promotional or publicity materials or for study and self-criticism. If the performer's career folds before he or she achieves fame, such photographs (as well as posters, banderillas and other items of material culture) tend to be treated as evidence of an ex-novillero's historical bullfighting identity and are used to represent the self and its memories. The initial stages of a bullfighting career are extremely precarious and future success is not assured. Every step tends to be marked by, and invested in, a photograph. Not only are performances photographed, but such photography collections may also be regarded as expressions of complete torero identities. For example, included in the collection of a woman ex-bullfighter were performance shots, portraits of her dressed in a suit of lights and also in a country suit, shots of her in taurine locations, pictures of her with artefacts, with co-performers, and in bullfighting clubs. On the one hand, associated with her identity as an ex-bullfighter, these image-documents were also treated as evidence that she possessed the knowledge that would justify her status as an aficionada. As photographers or photographees, both aficionadas and women bullfighters use photographs to express particular self-identities in the bullfighting world. However, their photographs are invested with different meanings as they are incorporated into different discourses and agendas. Thus the feminine identities these women intend to represent are not fixed within the image.

Those who assume that a 'woman's mind' cannot achieve a true understanding of the bullfight do not use the term aficionada simply to differentiate between biologically male and female bullfight devotees. Rather, they use gendered language to speak of a particular perspective on the bullfight. For many women who call themselves aficionadas, the term has a very different meaning. It does not refer to their commitment to playing a traditional feminine role in bullfighting. Instead they rate their afición as equal to that of any aficionado (regardless of biological sex). In this chapter I have labelled such women 'active aficionadas'. During my fieldwork it was evident that many women are committed to such an active involvement with bullfighting. They manifested this commitment in a range of different ways through their involvement in the bullfighting clubs, photography, journalism, etc. My research into televised bullfights (see Chapter 8), bullfighting photography and journalism suggests that women are actively engaged in the production of the cultural knowledge and material culture of contemporary bullfighting. 'Women' in general do not simply have hidden power in male-dominated bullfighting culture. Rather it is evident that many women wield different forms of public and private power: in economic terms, as cultural producers, and in the social and kinship relations of the world of bullfighting.

# Notes

1. In Córdoba a network of social and supporter bullfighting clubs – peñas or *tertulias* – thrives. These groups form contacts and alliances over a range of personal and public issues. They are registered and united under the Taurine Federation and the Federation of Peñas, and they are run by their own organising committees. Within Spanish anthropology attention has been focused on connections between associationism and local social structures and power networks (for example, Escalera 1991).

2. In 1993 one club organised a flight and a ten-day holiday in South America which incorporated two performances of Córdoba's top bullfighter in Mexico.

3. Some peñas represent specific social classes, and whilst people of varied social status can attend events at a peña based in an élite club, membership is limited to the upper classes.

4. Pérez Molina identifies certain differences between the emerging afición of youth and that of older and retired aficionados. He suggests that the 'new' aficionados tend to include those whose afición does not derive from family afición, but which has developed out of contemporary youth culture (1991: 450–1). This tendency will inevitably impact on the gender relations articulated in youth bullfighting culture.

5. Rather than manifesting the 'repressive' function which Sekula (1989) bases on the Foucauldian concept of surveillance.

6. Bullfighting performance imagery thus differs from sports photography which can be 'divided into two categories: winners and losers' and 'us and them' (Hagaman 1993: 49).

# Part 3

# Women Performers: From a Public Arena to a Domestic Screen

In Chapters 5 to 8 I shall focus on representations of women bullfighters. In Chapter 5 I will discuss media and experiential elements of women bullfighters' biographies and career structures. By concentrating on the progress, activities and social networks of particular performers I shall analyse how women performers may negotiate their identities in 'bullfighting culture'. In Chapter 6 some more specific strategies of self-representation are discussed in relation to how women bullfighters are categorised by different subjectivities. In Chapter 7 this theme is developed further through an assessment of how the debates for and against women bullfighters tend to be centred on female physiology. Finally, in Chapter 8 I shall consider how these discourses and debates are represented and interpreted in the media bullfight.

# Gender, Power and Access to the Arena: Media, Experience and Representations of Self

I concluded Chapter 4 by pointing out that women do not own a singular type of power in bullfighting, rather different women are empowered in a variety of ways. In this chapter I shall explore the success of contemporary women performers through a discussion of media and self-representations of biography and experience. Different women have varying degrees of access to resources of power related to, for example, finance, enchufes,[1] knowledge or experience.

During my fieldwork the very successful Cristina Sánchez took centre stage both in the media and in local discourses on women bullfighters. In the course of their discussions about women bullfighters in Córdoba my informants also drew from local knowledge and personal experience to incorporate their representations of Antoñita la Cordobesa into the debate. Other contemporary women performers tended not to be mentioned by name. My informants distinguished between women bullfighters who perform on foot and contemporary rejoneadoras, who perform on horseback. The rejoneo is not generally considered to be 'real' bullfighting. Two rejoneadoras featured in our discussions, Maria Sara, a French woman who is a leading performer, and Carmen de Córdoba, a woman with local Cordoban connections who is based in El Esquorial near to Madrid. Informants' references to historical women performers also included local, national and global sources. From recent history, the Spanish Maribel Atienza and Angela Hernandez featured. From earlier in the twentieth century, examples of the local woman Maria Gomez, the Peruvian Conchita Cintrón and the Spaniard Juanita Cruz predominated. I will discuss historical data in more detail in Chapter 6.

In the Prologue I introduced a Cordoban woman bullfighter named Antoñita. I will reconstruct below some of the experiences Antoñita related to tell a story of an aspiring woman bullfighter. This is not Antoñita's story, but my invention, dotted with the embellishments of writing and evocative of emotions that neither Antoñita nor her family and friends may ever have felt. It is framed partially with the narrative of a biographical tale of 'any bullfighter'. I call the woman in my story Lola, a name which was once mistakenly used to refer to Antoñita in a press article. Antoñita's trainer, Miguel, was the owner of an extensive collection of bullfighting paraphernalia, had performed as a novillero himself and was considered an expert on local bullfighting matters. In the story below he is represented by the name of Juan. The contributions of both Antoñita and Miguel, are inextricable from my narrative and important to my research, but I do not pretend that they live in my text.[2] I describe my own experience, but make no claim to theirs.

## Lola, La Cordobesa

Lola was not born into an aficionado family and her decision to become a bullfighter was greeted with little encouragement from her parents. Her father, acknowledging her determination, conceded to arrange some performances in nearby village festivals which were organised by an influential friend. Her mother (like 'any mother' in the classic bullfighter's biography) was opposed to Lola's bullfighting ambition, but whilst she was extremely worried she was never actively obstructive. Lola said that really her parents thought she was absolutely crazy to want to be a bullfighter. Later, when Lola began training to enter the police force her mother's reaction was coined in the terms of a question. Why did Lola always have to try to do men's work? – What was wrong with a feminine career?

Lola realised she wanted to be a bullfighter when she was eleven years old, when she tested out some cape passes on one of the milk cows her father had recently purchased. She later, by now aged twelve, began training at the bullfighting school which was held in the bullring in Córdoba. There she was often confronted with men who were unwilling to take her seriously or approve of her ambition. Although the ex-bullfighters who trained students at the bullfighting school were helpful, Lola felt that most opportunities were given to the boys. She was often not notified of occasions when the chance to practise with live animals or to be observed by potential managers arose. The caretaker of the ring quite bluntly told her that such opportunities are 'not for you', and he appeared quite deliberately to withhold information. After some months when Lola learnt about Juan[3] she left the bullfighting school to begin training with him. Superficially Juan represents a typical traditional working-class Cordoban. In his late fifties, he has a passion for flamenco, local fiestas and of course bullfighting – in short, a taste for traditional activities. However, unlike many other men of his age and social and cultural orientations, he believes that women can bullfight and describes those who think otherwise as 'sexist'. Juan sees no reason why women should not bullfight to as high a standard as men, and regards himself an expert on such matters. He does not ascribe fully to traditional discourse on gendered roles in the bullfighting world; rather, he selects those elements which appeal to his own taste and lifestyle. The particularities of his subjectivity are formed from a lifetime of biographical experience.

Juan has devoted his life to bullfighting, and makes it his business to be aware of everything that happens in the local bullfighting world. He lives with his mother, his wife and two of his daughters who are as yet unmarried in a modern flat about ten minutes' walk from the old house where he grew up, a *casa de vecinos*[4] now owned by his mother, and one of the few remaining houses in its street – most are uninhabited, derelict or demolished. The front two rooms house Juan's private collection of bullfighting artefacts in an impressive private museum which has been featured in press articles and a television documentary. The back kitchen is still used, in the patio rabbits, chickens and other animals are kept and on the roof vegetables are grown. Juan has converted the plot of land opposite into a practice bullring where aspiring bullfighters sometimes train and where Juan has organised bullfighting schools to give voluntary help to those who, like Lola, want to become bullfighters.

Juan himself wanted to be a bullfighter and performed once in Córdoba as a novillero. He kept copies of the poster announcing his performance and is proud that he is listed in the *Cossío* bullfighting encyclopaedia. Despite (like most would-be toreros) failing to become a bullfighter, Juan remained inside the bullfighting world, working on a seasonal basis as part of the mule team that drags the dead bull out of the arena. Most of his time is spent in bullfighting clubs and arranging his own collection. Locally Juan is well known, his collection is a local resource from which items are proudly lent for exhibitions and it is visited by people seeking documentation.

Although Juan's social network in the bullfighting world is extensive, he is not influential in upper-class social circles and his financial resources are limited. Juan became Lola's trainer, manager, swords handler and friend. His wife and daughters also extended the emotional support and encouragement that it was difficult for her own family to offer. However, Juan's marginal relationship to the power networks that would have given Lola a good start in bullfighting barred access to other crucial resources. Neither Juan nor Lola had the money necessary to buy live animals or organise promotional fights.

Lola spent a further four years living and training at a bullfighting school in a Cordoban village, but after dedicating eight years of her life to bullfighting she relinquished her ambition. Lack of sponsorship, parental pressure and insufficient contracts had eventually led her to 'give up': a decision based on hours of deliberation, tears and, above all, the strength required to abandon one's dream. In more practical terms she had no manager nor funds to promote herself. She had invested immeasurable time and energy in her training – the total involvement and dedication that bullfighting demands of its performers means that those who leave do not simply switch careers, but must start to build a new life, often having neglected their schooling and in possession of few academic certificates.

## Putting up Pictures: charting success

The visual dimensions of performance and bullfighting culture play an important role in discourses about women performers. For example, as I show in the Prologue, informants tended to visualise reputation when speaking of Antoñita. Their critiques inscribed intention in her visual appearance: 'She looked like she thought . . .', 'She walked around as if she . . .'. Similarly, approval was granted through a visualisation that referred to a material artwork which local discourse uses to speak of moral virtue. These instances indicate how material, embodied and oral accounts become interwoven in everyday negotiations and constructions of reality. All of this indicates how the visual dimension of a bullfighting career must be carefully managed.

Visual images formed part of the career narrative presented to me by both Antoñita and her trainer's family.[5] Antoñita's photographs, presented in a small album, were mainly taken during her performances. They included public bullfights, a sequence from a ganadería where young bulls and cows were being tested, and others were from a *capea* (a country bullfighting fiesta) just outside the city of Córdoba. Antoñita lamented the lack of close-ups, and self-criticism dominated her commentaries. It seemed to me that initially these images had served as a tool for self-reflection and 'improvement' in the personal project of this bullfighter. When they were shown to me, several years later, they were invested with further meanings as they had become the focus of a lament for what 'could have been', the production of memory, and a 'document' of what had been.

The collection included portrait shots of Antoñita dressed in her traje de luces (suit of lights). When we met she was considering selling this expensive item. The costume is not only a prerequisite for performing, but it is also invested with a deeper significance.[6] A torero is visualised dressed in a traje de luces, to wear it is tantamount to declaring one's intention to perform. Furthermore, the traje can stand as a landmark in the narrative of a performer's success story: a particular suit of lights can be used to invoke memories of an occasion, achievement, one performance or a whole era. Antoñita's plans to sell her suit become more significant when one considers the convention of collecting trajes.[7]

Costume is an important medium for the representation of self. Antoñita said she considered it important that one dress appropriately even when training. She harshly criticised a girl who trained wearing a bikini during the high summer temperatures (over 40°C) in Córdoba. Antoñita considered shorts and a T-shirt appropriate even in such temperatures. Similarly, a girl at the bullfighting school demonstrated some cape passes for me one evening when she hadn't dressed to train; she said she felt and looked ridiculous training in a skirt. Whilst neither a skirt nor bikini present technical obstacles to performing cape passes, correct dress is important if one's bullfighting ambition is to be taken seriously. This is especially significant for women since they are often presumed to be less serious in their aspirations than their male counterparts.

Antoñita employed conventional visual strategies. She dressed correctly and used her photographs in established channels of publicity. Miguel helped to ensure that Antoñita was well placed on the visual map of the bullfighting world. He used his network of contacts in Córdoba's peñas to hang framed black and white shots of Antoñita in triumphant poses in several wall-displays. Antoñita was located in the bullfighting history of Córdoba, not only through

Miguel's work, but also in press reports and in her televised performance in the 'Becerrada Homenaje a la Mujer Cordobesa'. The strikingly unusual element in this example, is the connection between the bullfight and a female body implied by both the material images and by her physical presence.

### Why did Antoñita fail?: sex, gender, power and context

Antoñita stressed two conditions necessary for her success. First, a training in theory and practice such as that provided at the Madrid Bullfighting School. Second, a patron with the power, influence and resources needed to organise public performances and secure contracts. It is difficult for a woman to come across such support; the few sponsors willing to invest in the future of a bullfighter tend to support promising boys. Even those who believe that a woman bullfighter merits support are faced with the possibility of receiving no return on their investments; financial security alone cannot avoid the many additional obstacles which confront women.

Antoñita's inability to achieve her goal need not be classified as failure either anthropologically or locally. Indeed, for those who view women's bullfighting as a novelty, her serious ambition is regarded as a silly feminine excursion. Antoñita's lack of practical, economic and emotional encouragement from the key figures in local bullfighting was related to her biological sex. Her inability to find a patron was inevitably linked with how economic strategies are influenced by dominant discourses in the bullfighting world. An individual's skill and potential are often graded in ways which are contingent upon the sex of the performer (see Chapter 7). For example, when some informants insisted that women could not perform with *arte* they were referring to the relationships between different types of bravery, fear and intelligence; and to the distinction between art and spectacle. It was assumed that women bullfighters cannot experience masculine fear, and therefore they cannot overcome their fear through the combination of intelligence, bravery and sensitivity that results in the production of art. The relationship between art and bravery in this line of thought can be illustrated by one informant's comparison of two male bullfighters: one, he commented, was very brave, but lacked intelligence, the other had the opposite problem, he was intelligent and capable of producing art on occasion, but unfortunately was not brave. Here a connection was set up between art and intelligence. My informant's perspective dictated that whilst bravery cannot create an artistic performance, it is bravery alone which creates spectacle.

The gender role segregation model that dominates traditional bullfighting discourse, appears to have some practical implications for the way in which women bullfighters experience their careers. In the early 1990s this model suggested that women were unable to perform artistically, or be successful (i.e. high earning and continually performing) bullfighters, thus discouraging patrons from making a commitment to a woman. It was pointed out to me that even when a potential patron considers women to be just as capable as men, the 'evidence' presented by women's experience makes a woman bullfighter an unconvincing financial investment. This kind of vicious circle serves as an experienced limiting force for women who aspire to be bullfighters. When someone with the power, economic backing and desire to disprove the traditionalist interpretation invests in a woman performer such restrictions and limitations may be lifted. Antoñita and Miguel lacked the power and economic resources necessary to accomplish such a feat.

Those informants who wanted to construct a positive and complimentary image of Antoñita represented her as a nice, attractive Cordoban girl who had tried to be a bullfighter and had performed several times, but had been confronted with the relatively common difficulty of a lack of funds and a patron. They pointed out that this problem was greatly magnified by her being a woman, and thus their account would come to a close with a sad shrug of the shoulders. However, the other version which was related by those who wished to represent women bullfighters in a negative light, portrayed Antoñita as an ugly threat to the natural order. Her morality and her femininity were brought into question as were her motives for wishing to be successful – she was accused of having egotistical aspirations to self-glorification, and of not being a genuine aficionada. Her failure, in this account, was thus explained by her pretence, her lack of true afición as evidenced by her non-conformity to the rules which dictate that the correct expression of feminine afición is to adopt the role of spectator. In these ways her reputation and integrity were questioned.

## Gender, Culture and Success/Failure

Not all local explanations of women's failure to succeed as bullfighters were based on a binary distinction between male and female biology and personality. A nature/culture debate also emerged in local discussion[8] – some informants defined the problems women encounter as 'cultural'. A retired bullfighter teaching at the bullfighting school attributed the barriers which men construct against women performers to 'the continuation of Spain's sexist past into the present'. For him the contemporary situation is the result of many years of an authoritarian government which had left the Spanish people subservient to the extent that even the last twenty years of freedom had not changed their attitudes. He cited many examples to back up his argument that women can perform as well as men. He attributed 'the problem' of people's opposition to women performers to the franquist period during which men had come to see women as 'different' and to feel obliged to treat them 'carefully'. For this reason, he explained, he found training women problematic since it was impossible to say the same things to a woman as one would to a man in a man-to-man conversation. For example, women must be criticised more gently – he felt unable either to tell a woman she was useless at bullfighting or to call her names.[9] Other informants and journalists seemed to have similar points of view with regard to women's bullfighting ability. For example, Baeza (1992) identifies the problem for women bullfighters as the fact that 'behind the bull's horns there is a public who will not excuse a bad performance'. Also, Villan points out that it was her male colleagues who were most likely to wound Cristina Sánchez. He quotes the bullfighter Belmonte's idea that rather than brute strength and force, it is the intelligence and art of the bullfighter that controls the bull, thus he argues that there is no reason why Cristina Sánchez should not triumph (Villan 1993: 6). These perspectives see gender as culturally constructed, and they claim that the assumption that biological sex differences restrict women's physiological and intellectual capacity to perform is a mistaken one. Many people are happy to accept women performers, but in the early 1990s most had no vested interest in pressing for change.

Whilst public representations and discourses on gender affect the opportunities available to aspiring women bullfighters, kinship and social networking, or enchufe's, also merit consideration. To return to the example of Lola: whilst she struggled against the odds to become a bullfighter, Lola received no encouragement from her own family and relied greatly on her allies in the bullfighting world for emotional backup. Her mother did not withdraw all support – she attended some performances and accompanied her daughter to hospital when she was injured. Her father was neither sufficiently powerful or involved in bullfighting to further her career, and family networks did not provide the often vital link between a young bullfighter and the bullfighting world. Lola's family had no aficionado identity or history.

In addition to the practical benefits of kinship ties for social networking, being the male 'blood relative' of a bullfighter offers another significant advantage; bullfighting skill and understanding is commonly believed to be inherited (reproduced biologically) along the male line whilst women supposedly assimilate afición through socialisation in bullfighting circles (see Chapter 4). However, it is often the case that the notion of an inheritance of some intrinsic compatibility with bullfighting is extended to female offspring. At the very least, being closely related to a male bullfighter adds to a woman's credibility and possibilities. In contrast to Lola's experience, the case of Cristina Sánchez, whose father is a banderillero with a long-term involvement in bullfighting, shows how kinship connections can contribute to an entirely more positive experience. The kind of enchufe relationships which extend from the family into the bullfighting world were simply not available to Lola. In Córdoba the limited resources which were available for aspiring bullfighters were far beyond her social scope. Indeed, the dominant local constructions of Cordoban bullfighting history locate kinship connections at the very centre of bullfighting success. One commentator claims that all bullfighters in Córdoba are related by kinship (Mira 1984), and informants referred to the bullfighters of Córdoba as 'one big family'; frequently they spoke of performers in terms of their kinship connections with other local bullfighters. The example of the supposedly illegitimate son of the retired bullfighter El Cordobés demonstrates how legitimate, or recognised paternity is not required (here the alleged father refuses to acknowledge his son) in order for the connection to lend one authenticity. In this case, the physical similarity and shared bullfighting skill between 'father' and 'son' served to give the young El Cordobés a much needed boost of publicity. On the other hand, it proved impossible for Lola to break into a bullfighting world in which kinship links are instrumental in gaining access to vital resources, and where descriptions of the bullfighters who belong to this world are often voiced in terms of kinship. Whilst not all successful local bullfighters are related by kin, a substantial number are; thus the myth is perpetuated and the connections maintained.

I shall now turn to the career of Cristina Sánchez, hers is a success story. The purpose of juxtaposing these accounts of two young women of about the same age, who are both attempting to launch themselves as bullfighters at around the same time in different parts of Spain is not to set up a typology of success versus failure. Rather, I intend to describe two examples of the contexts of success and failure.[10]

## A Foot in the Ring and a Feature in the Media

The media narrative of the success of Cristina Sánchez forms an integral element of the story it represents. Her initial triumphs inspired an abundance of press and journal reports which focused on Cristina herself and the so-called history of women bullfighters in which she was set up as 'the latest'. This initial flare of publicity stemmed from Cristina winning the 'best student' competition at the Madrid Bullfighting School, which by implication proved her superiority to her male contemporaries. In the words of one journal, 'she went to the bullfighting school just like any other guy' (6 Toros 6 (II), 1992). The media discourse on Cristina's success became woven into Antoñita's account insofar as she identified the Madrid School as a place where she may have been able to succeed. The media printed Cristina's name alongside those of the famous; and the initial recommendation of ex-bullfighter Gregorio Sánchez, her trainer at the school, was instrumental in beginning her career. Her ensuing performances were well documented and she was sometimes dedicated more space in print than the novilleros with whom she shared the ring. For example, when Cristina appeared in 1992 alongside Miguel Antonio Alcoba and Paco Ortega, both sons of famous bullfighters, she was given a more lengthy and praise-filled report (for example in M.T 1992 N°1.271 p22). Cristina was frequently photographed – when performing, when training, in her casual clothes and in hospital. This diversity of images suited those informants who wanted to 'see what she's like' so as to get a sense of 'who she is'. Most men and women commented on her 'attractive' appearance saying they had expected her to be 'butch'. Some women especially admired Cristina's highlighted blonde hair and immaculate eye make-up – they approved of both the performer and the person.

Reviews of Cristina were positive. Some traditionalist informants shrugged this detail off, remarking that it would be too unkind to print the cruel truth about the low quality of a woman's performance. Many others who had seen her perform were impressed, but they disagreed over whether or not she demonstrated *arte*. It was conceded that she displayed bravery of different types, but often the granting of such a quality was tempered by the qualification that it still was not 'the same' as seeing a male bullfighter perform. Thus I found that approval was forthcoming but it was usually justified from a range of different standpoints.

During the season of 1992 there was much speculation over when Cristina would graduate to perform with picadores. When she did so in February 1993 in a small village named Valdemorillo (in the Madrid Province) a fresh surge of publicity and reportage was initiated. Cristina had already received good reviews from her season in Latin America and her publicity shots had been splashed over the covers of the leading bullfighting weeklies (*Aplausos; El Ruedo*). All her injuries and performances had been reported on in detail, mainly in newspapers and journals but also on television and several of her performances had been transmitted live from Latin America. Sometimes Cristina's activities became obscured by public and conversational debate. For example, after suffering an injury in Latin America she cancelled a subsequent performance. Whilst Cristina publicly insisted that her doctors would not permit her to perform, media controversy developed over claims that she had cancelled out of fear of being gored again. The rumours were only dispelled on her successful return to the ring. Some informants, rather than engaging in the debate, shrugged off the issue, pointing out rather superciliously that these are exactly the kinds of discourse that one could expect to develop amongst (other) aficionados and the media.

The progression to performing with picadores is a significant achievement that Antoñita did not manage. By this point in her career however, Cristina was under the management of French businessman André Viard. Her potential for success had been well publicised, her performances had drawn the crowds and she had therefore been able to attract a sponsor. The reports on her début were positive and wide-ranging but many were a reflection upon Cristina's novelty status as much as a belief in real bullfighting merit. Most male bullfighters' début with picadores pass unnoticed outside their own circles, such undivided press attention tends only to be received once a bullfighter has performed successfully with picadores for some time. In contrast, Cristina's performance featured in *El*

*Mundo* magazine (a six-page colour article) in Spain and reached, amongst others, the *Guardian* in England, and the *Jakarta Post* in Indonesia. During the two weeks following this performance Cristina was constructed and reconstructed in different media which purported to inform the nation and beyond about the woman, the issues and her possibilities for the future. Media coverage soon died down however, and Cristina was left to follow a more normal routine of training and performances 'like any other novillero'. Throughout she maintained her position amongst the top ten *novilleros* in the weekly listings.

Media reports on Cristina have been quite diverse but the key aspects of her representation can be summed up as follows: Cristina, aged twenty (in 1993), is the daughter of a banderillero and a star student of the Madrid Bullfighting School. She receives strong parental support, despite motherly worries, and her father is her day-to-day trainer. Cristina is serious, dedicated, determined and talented – there is no reason why she should not succeed (this point was also reiterated to me in conversation with her father) and she now has an influential manager. Furthermore, Cristina pertains to a (supposed) long history of women's bullfighting (see Chapter 9). Photographic representations of Cristina present her in poses that stand for triumph, success, seriousness, and ability in action. In 1994 the question of whether she would ever graduate to full torero status remained an issue for debate in the media and amongst my informants. The main reference points in these media constructions of Cristina and her biography compare significantly with traditionalist models of bullfighters and their career narratives. They describe her as fulfilling the main criteria for success. Although Cristina is a woman she has been conceded the following important attributes: kin support and networks in the bullfighting world; the correct attitude, intelligence, skill and a potential for success, a manager and a sponsor. The instances of this media image have been broad-based, ranging from the gossip magazines, serious newspapers and bullfighting journals. In interview, public speaking and discussion, Cristina presents a similar self-image. This is crucial because a bullfighter is a public figure; in public, reputation and integrity must be maintained. When a bullfighter speaks or gives question and answer sessions in public he/she often finds him/herself in a confrontational situation. It is important that the performer defend him/herself appropriately in public to maintain his/her reputation as a person capable of dealing with such demanding situations, and to reaffirm his/her public image and identity. Whilst most anthropologists of Spain have associated such representations with a concept of masculine honour,[11] the defence of reputation in public confrontation is evidently not exclusively a concern of men. Not only women bullfighters, but women politicians, business women, and other women who work in the public domain are obliged to deal with such situations in the everyday maintenance of reputations and integrities. The media image of a woman bullfighter is particularly important because traditional bullfight discourse asserts that the life of a bullfighter is not a suitable or pleasant lifestyle for a woman. As one informant, the wife of an ex-bullfighter told me, 'this life is not comfortable or glamorous, you are always travelling from city to city, and during the bullfighting season you almost live out of a chain of different hotels, you often have to spend the night travelling and sleeping in the car'.

## Access and Allies

I have described some of the difficulties faced by women attempting to break into bullfighting. Most women bullfighters have a male ally in the bullfighting world. The socialising in exclusively male circles in bars, the masculine camaraderie, the exchanging of dirty jokes, and the like are all difficult for a woman to participate in. Not because women necessarily find this behaviour offensive, but because many men, especially those who informants have referred to as the 'traditionalists' refuse to make this type of social contact with women – they use different vocabulary and metaphors when in the company of women. This restricts women's access to the *confianza* needed to create and manipulate social contacts in the bullfighting world. Participation in these networks can be crucial for gathering information about performance and practice opportunities. Clearly the information is much more accessible to men, and through male allies women can overcome some of the problems related to the allocation of access to power and information according to sex. To a certain extent a woman's possibilities depend on the influence held by her male representative.[12] Through her father Cristina Sánchez was well connected to the networks that are especially important for a beginner, whereas Antoñita had no powerful ally in the Cordoban networks. I heard of several girls who were deterred after a few performances; who were unable to make the 'big break' necessary to fuel their careers towards success. A curious story is that of a Dutch woman who worked in a Cordoban gymnasium to support herself whilst training to bullfight. Lacking insider contacts in Córdoba's bullfighting world and relatively unknown in bullfighting circles, she never performed in the city and shortly moved on. It was said that she had taken a job as a tattoo artist in Algeciras – such a classification of her activities is akin to the frequent marginalisation of women's bullfighting.

Cristina's success and the progression of women's bullfighting to the forefront of the media attention in the mid 1990s must be understood as occurring interdependently rather than in causal sequence. The increasing acceptability and heightened commercial potential of other women bullfighters who, in 1996, progressed further through the league tables introduces another variable. In 1996 Cristina was the first woman bullfighter to graduate to full professional status in Europe by taking the alternativa (in Nîmes, May 1996), and later performing with full-grown bulls in Spain. During the 1996 season she remained a popular matador de toros. Her success has been represented by a multi-stranded media narrative taken up by television, news, bullfight media and more recently gossip magazines. Men performers have been publicly obliged to determine where they wish to stand in relation to her, and their positions have often been couched in binary terms of rejection or acceptance of contracts to perform alongside her. In this sense Cristina's success has involved a reconfiguration of the public/media domain of bullfighting. A high-profile example of how public identities have come to be negotiated in a consumer culture has emerged in the case of her treatment by two leading young toreros: El Cordobés[13] and Jesulín de Ubrique. Several bullfighters have refused to perform with Cristina and their protests have often been well publicised. Since her graduation to full matador status attention has turned to the denial of her credibility which has been voiced by the top performer Jesulín de Ubrique, a 24-year-old media hero, labelled the 'women's bullfighter'. He is quoted as saying, 'I don't believe women can be professional bullfighters' and is credited with the words, 'I don't like at all to see a woman working when her work stops her from looking after her husband, children and home as she ought to' (*Tiempo*, 20 July 1996: 107–8). In May 1996 Jesulín set himself in direct opposition to Cristina, as a man who performs for women and as one of the few remaining performers who would not share the arena with her. By July 1996 El Cordobés, who had recently taken the lead from Jesulín in the league ratings formed an

**Figure 16:** The cover of the weekly *Semana* magazine, 17 July 1996

opportune alliance with Cristina; they began a series of extremely successful double-bill performances. Flattering reviews were accompanied by a front-page feature in *Semana* (17 July 1996) a magazine considered by most to be of the genre of women's 'gossip' magazines, and one of the favourite publications of Jesulín's audience. Curiously, in the issue of the leading bullfight magazine *Aplausos* on sale the same week (8 July 1996) Jesulín sought to resituate himself: 'I personally have never said that I wouldn't perform with her . . . I will perform with her when the time comes and for now I congratulate her because she has demonstrated that she has much merit'. The journalist suggested that Jesulín's manager had instigated the refusal. 'Of course,' said one informant, 'bullfighters only ever say what they are told to.'

## A Wave or a Storm?

Historical accounts of women's bullfighting have tended to identify 'waves' or eras of women's bullfighting, represented by outbursts of activity followed by a relative absence of women performers. Juanita Cruz is named as the leading light of the 1930s, whereas for the 1970s Angela and Maribél[14] share centre stage. This historicisation has in part been exacerbated by the prohibitions placed on women performers during the twentieth century (see Chapter 6). In the media narrative of the 1990s Cristina Sánchez is represented as the leading figure whilst a series of lesser women performers rise in her wake. These women who are stepping into the limelight in the 1990s tend to follow similar career paths. Yolanda Caravajal, Mari Paz Vega, Raquel Castelló and Laura Valencia (who attended the same school as Cristina in Madrid) have all passed through bullfighting schools where they received formal training. Mari Paz Vega is, like Cristina, the daughter of a novillero, Francisco Vega, and the sister of a banderillero and three novilleros. Whilst the careers of these women are documented in Feiner's 'history' (1995), and their performances are reported in the standard format, they do not receive the degree of media attention which is showered on Cristina. However, the general career pattern that these women follow and their uses of kinship and other networks appears similar to that of both Cristina Sánchez and their male colleagues. This suggests that these women, and others, participate in a structured career narrative which has already been established for male performers; whilst their biological sex may be considered novel in the world of bullfighting, the routes by which they enter its domain are not.

The connections of kinship are similarly stressed in aficionado and media discourses about horseback bullfighters. The French rejoneadora Maria Sara is the daughter of actors but the partner of a ganadero, Carmen de Córdoba is the daughter of a rejoneador, and the Portuguese Marta Manuela is the daughter of a horse-dealer with connections in Portuguese bullfighting networks (Sardo 1996). These connections and enchufes make available livestock, and training and performance opportunities. Weekend newspaper supplements, bullfighting journals and the gossip press appear sympathetic to contemporary women performers. This positive representation and the advantages which I have described above have contributed greatly to the development of some women's careers as bullfighters in the 1990s. However, this account of the progress of some women should be contextualised by a wider understanding of the range of subjectivities that militate for and against women bullfighters. In the following chapter I will focus on terminology and costume to discuss how these have been incorporated into contemporary and historical standpoints on women performers. In Chapter 7 I will explore how these subjectivities interpret the physical bodies of women performers.

## Notes

1. Enchufes are one's influential social contacts. The term is derived from the verb, *enchufar*- literally to 'plug in'.
2. This strategy is employed in an attempt to resolve the very difficult issue of writing about the lives and ambitions of people who are not 'media figures' – they do not expect to be 'misrepresented'.
3. The information came from a teenage boy who was training with Juan. He left Juan for the bullring and became a moderately successful novillero with financial backing from his family and a bullfighting club who supported him.
4. *Casa de vecinos* translates literally as a 'house of neighbours'. Earlier in the twentieth century this was a typical form of cheap accommodation. Each family occupied a room and shared cooking facilities and usually a patio (courtyard) with other families. Most families who lived in casas de vecinos have now been rehoused in blocks of flats.
5. My conversations with Miguel sometimes centred around collections of photographs from Antoñita's career.

6. The embroidered traje de luces is handmade by specialist tailors. Ownership, rather than renting, of a suit signifies one's entry into bullfighting. To say that one will *vestirse de luces* is tantamount to announcing that one will perform.

7. The bullfighting museum in Córdoba housed an exhibition of suits of lights during my fieldwork. Exhibits over a hundred years old were volunteered by the families of the bullfighters from whom they had been inherited.

8. The phrase, 'The bull doesn't distinguish between men and women,' neatly illustrates a multiplicity of ways of interpreting the nature/culture and gender binaries of discourses about bullfighting. This observation may support quite different standpoints. For example as part of the commentary of a televised bullfight in which Cristina Sánchez performed it was employed as a dramatic device to emphasise that the bull would make no concessions. It is sometimes used to state that since a bull does not realise that women must be treated more gently than men, bullfighting is too dangerous for women. However, a woman bullfighter used the phrase to argue that sexual equality was recognised by the bull, but not by humans; therefore, through bullfighting equality could be proven since the bull had no prejudiced bias against her sex. The latter interpretation entails a critique of culture proposing that non-discrimination is 'natural' and more useful than the cultural 'artificial' construction of gender.

9. A woman who had attended the school to train as a serious bullfighter told me that the teachers at the bullfighting school had treated her less seriously than the male students. They had been happier to talk and joke with her rather than offer her the concentrated tuition that she needed. Several other young women attended the bullfighting school with the intention of improving their bullfighting knowledge, rather than in order to become bullfighters. In contrast, their presence at the bullfighting school was non-problematic for their male peers and the tutors alike.

10. Mitchell usefully suggests that an examination of the 'failures' of the bullfight may reveal more than a focus which concentrates solely on the published biographies of the successful (1991: 96). However, Mitchell's larger project is inherently problematic: he creates a model of a character type of the successful bullfighter and concludes that successful performers are by definition masochists (1991: 103).

11. Marvin describes public confrontations in terms of 'honour'. He stresses the importance of 'reputation' in conditions where people have to resort to self-help because they cannot rely on the State. He writes, 'what is at stake in the competitive relations between men in such systems is reputation – which is something that is accorded to an individual *by others*' (1986: 125). Marvin argues that the bullfight plays out the 'ideal behaviour' required of men when they are involved in public confrontations – when confronted a man must prove his readiness not to back down. 'If the matador is able to meet the challenge successfully he gains prestige and

status, and vindicates his claim to be a true man. Failure brings insult, ridicule and a loss of reputation' (ibid.: 1986: 126). This notion of honour is more useful than the honour–shame model discussed in Chapter 2.

12. A similar system also works for male bullfighters, but at the initial stages of a career a man has greater scope for self-management.

13. This younger El Cordobés claims to be the illegitimate son of his older namesake. The alleged father however denies any connection.

14. The father of 1970s performer Maribel Atienza worked in a bullring, her mother was 'an aficionada' (*Estar Viva* 188, 31 May–6 June 1992).

# Toreras and Trajes: Dressing Up in the Names of Histories

## 'Logical' Dress Sense and Biological Sex?

Early in 1993 I attended Cristina Sánchez's *debút con picadores* in Valdemorillo, Madrid. On my return to Córdoba two elderly aficionados approached me. They were curious about her performance. One asked me if she had worn a traje de luces. 'I wanted to know,' he said, responding to my puzzled expression, 'because in the past toreras used to perform wearing a long skirt.' His companion compared such an outfit to the suit that women used to wear to ride sidesaddle.

Having attended one of her performances the previous year I had personally expected Cristina to wear a traje de luces nevertheless, amongst aficionados, controversy exists over the correctness of this costume. Unlike some aficionados, these elderly men agreed approvingly that Cristina's traje would offer her more mobility, and they suggested that long skirts had made bullfighting more difficult and dangerous for women in the past. One of them concluded that it was perfectly 'logical' that, in the 1990s, women should perform in trousers – as he pointed out I was wearing trousers and it seemed that these days most women did. The historical references these men had called upon were related to local historical knowledge and entailed an interweaving of biography and experience with bullfight history. It transpired that one of them was the son of a man who, in the 1930s, managed the career of Maria Gomez a Cordoban woman performer. He told me that Maria Gomez, like some of her contemporaries, did perform wearing a skirt. Their version of the history of bullfighting costume is supported by Doré's (1862) drawing of Teresa Bolsí (see, for example, Valverde 1992). This image, in my experience, represents the most frequently referenced icon in

**Figure 17:** Teresa Bolsí (Gustavo Doré )

accounts of a historical tradition of women's bullfighting. It depicts a woman wearing a crinoline dress standing triumphantly over a dead bull. However, it is not certain that Teresa Bolsí performed in her crinoline – little more is known of her (see Boada and Cebolla 1986; Feiner 1995) than the accounts that have been constructed around, and invested in, her image. Further historical research indicates that the costumes tended to vary amongst women. Whilst for men the traje de luces (or alternatively the traje corto for less formal events) was the only appropriate option, women performers were presented with a wider range of choices.

Different costumes will be made meaningful by aficionados in particular ways, seemingly regardless of the wearer's intention. In this chapter I shall focus on how costume is worn, invoked and imagined to express difference and/or sameness between categories of performer. In doing so I will consider how particular meanings are invested in dressed bodies. In particular, I shall explore the way relationships between costume, biological sex and gender are constructed to express perspectives on women bullfighters. Costume as it is fitted to, and in a sense becomes part of, the sexed body becomes inextricably connected to gender identity. I aim to develop this theme by asking how subjectivities and material culture intersect in the expression of selves and others in relation to both the gender invested in a traje de luces and/or the gender ambiguity attributed to the woman wearing it. The combination of a traje de luces and a female body is problematised or reconciled in a variety of different ways. Moreover in many cases it was considered entirely appropriate – a standpoint which will be considered in relation to the wider context of fashion and sports wear. In my following analysis of terminology I draw on similar themes to examine how language can become both gender-ambiguous and laden with new meaning depending upon who is saying what about women bullfighters. During my fieldwork both what women bullfighters should wear and the title by which they should be referred to became issues in aficionado discussions and media representations. Various standpoints frequently sought to attach women bullfighters to particular histories or traditions of bullfighting. I propose to situate interpretations of women performers in relation to contemporary language and fashion.

## The Historical Tradition of Women's Bullfighting: an ambiguous claim to legitimacy[1]

On 17 August 1993 the Spanish television channel TVE1 transmitted a bullfight from Zaragoza featuring two rejoneadores, the Portuguese *forçados* and (then) novillera Cristina Sánchez. This was a significant combination in itself since it involved three non-mainstream categories of performers. When Cristina's bull entered the arena the commentator began to relate 'the history of women's bullfighting', commencing (in this instance) with La Pajulera of the 1770s,[2] and continuing with the observation that most women, except Juanita Cruz, had performed only in minor festivals. The visual narrative of Cristina's performance thus shared its media context with the oral historical narrative of the 'tradition of women bullfighters'. By the time Cristina was preparing for the kill – the key moment of the performance, the speaker had arrived at La Reverte to relate a tale (see below) about how a man had performed in the first decade of this century disguised as a woman. This accompaniment continued whilst Cristina finally put the bull to death.

A few months previous to this media bullfight, in March 1993, Cristina Sánchez visited Córdoba, to present a lecture based on her experiences entitled 'The Presence of Women in the bullfight'. She was introduced by a local public speaker, who situated her in a way by now familiar to me. He took as his starting point the 'appearance' of women in the bullrings of nineteenth-century Spain, and then he proceeded to speak of La Fragosa (1830s), La Garbancera(1890s) La Guerrita (1880s–1890s), La Reverte (1910s), Juanita Cruz (1930s), Conchita Cintrón (1940s–1950s) and Maribel Atienza (1970s). These same women took centre stage in various magazine features. For instance, in 1992, at the initial stages of construction of the 'media woman bullfighter' journalist Joaquín Vidal writes:

> Her ancestors are Angela and Maribel Atienza, but the veteran aficionados remember Conchita Cintrón the rejoneadora of the 1940s who when she set her feet on the ground performed better than many bullfighters of her time. Cristina Sánchez, whose ambition is to make herself a figure in bullfighting finds herself in the same line. And she's already on the way. (Vidal 1992)

The flurry of media attention that followed Cristina's success tended to follow two narratives. The first, described in the previous chapter locates her in mainstream bullfighting. The second, discussed in this chapter situates her as the most recent character in a nineteenth-

and twentieth-century history of women bullfighters. The latter construction involves the invention of a history of women bull-fighters. My understanding is that this particular version of history has developed partially as a response to the contemporary news-worthiness of women bullfighters. The compulsion to identify Cristina with a single history is equally apparent in academic work, where attempts to situate women bullfighters have seldom deviated from this form of genealogy. In Córdoba, González Viñas reflected on the historic cases of Teresa Bolsí, La Pajulera, La Reverte, Petra Kobloski, and Conchita Cintrón in an attempt to explain why women cannot succeed in bullfighting (1992: 10). These sequences, like the histories of Boada and Cebolla, and Feiner assume historical continuity between contemporary women bullfighters and those who were active either one hundred or sixty years ago. Similarly, Pitt-Rivers (1993: 14–15) attributes the success of Cristina Sánchez and other contemporary and historic women bullfighters to their shared symbolic value as a Joan of Arc figure, thereby placing these rather different performers in a single category of 'woman'. More recently, MacClancey, whilst recognising that contemporary women attempt to distinguish themselves from their 'predecessors' (1996: 74) has outlined a similar version of their 'history' to argue that his 'brief list of female bullfighters over the last three centuries demonstrates the persistence of the tradition' (1996: 73). This idea of historical continuity is of some relevance. Successive government prohibitions did create a distinct category of 'women bullfighters' which existed within the terminology of their political discourse. It is likely that this category was also incorporated by other discourses (apart from those I cite above). However, the exclusive category, of 'women bullfighters' is also very restricting for an anthropological analysis and I suggest that a range of different interpretations of women bullfighters can be better realised through a questioning of the absolute existence of a continuing historical tradition of women performers.

The so-called historical tradition of women's bullfighting is effectively distinguished from another different history of male/mainstream bullfighting, therefore establishing an essentialist dichotomy of masculine and feminine traditions in bullfighting. The accounts cited above seem to assume that any contemporary bullfighter who is female pertains to the feminine tradition, thus neatly disassociating her from mainstream bullfighting. Whilst accounts drawn from this (invented) tradition are often intended to justify the contemporary presence of women in the name of tradition, in a sense these polemics are self-effacing insofar as because they justify contemporary women performers in terms of a historical tradition which is marginalised by the mainstream activity they aspire to participate in. The 'of course women can bullfight . . . they have *always* been bullfighters' standpoint is then open to the retort that 'but they've never been *real* bullfighters, and they *never will be'* – an exchange I heard repeated several times by different people during my fieldwork.

I found that in order to understand representations of women performers it was significant to consider how these representations were related to classifications of women bullfighters in terms of their sameness or difference to other bullfighters. Firstly, women bullfighters of the past; secondly other contemporary novelty or 'non-serious' performers; and thirdly contemporary men bull-fighters. Different subjectivities thus make the gender of women performers ambiguous, safe or normal in different ways, and to a certain extent these classifications depended upon which history they were placed in by any one text, television commentary, or aficionado conversation. For instance, constructions of historical continuity between contemporary and historical women bullfighters served to resolve the ambiguous gender of contemporary women performers by identifying them with an historically feminised bullfight (which was recognised as an appropriate feminine activity by some). Such accounts are easily assimilated by traditional discourse since they represent gender role segregation. Nevertheless, the claim for historical continuity is unstable. In an either/or scenario where women bullfighters were obliged to assume one rather than several histories it could be argued that their links to their 'predecessors' are rather tenuous. In practice however, some informants perceived there to be no inconsistency in calling upon this 'history' to justify the contemporary presence of women in mainstream bullfighting.

### Dressed with Meanings

A flick through the visual histories of women's bullfighting constructed by Boada and Cebolla (1986) and Feiner (1995)[3] reveals a series of women posing in trajes de luces. For example, the 1880s performer La Fragosa was sketched in the bullring dressed in a full traje de luces,[4] and publicity photographs of a whole *cuadrilla de*

**Figure 18:** Cristina Sánchez performing in her *traje de luces* Valdemorillo 1993
© Sarah Pink

*señoritas toreras* (team of women bullfighters) wearing suits of lights exist from the end of the nineteenth century (see Boada and Cebolla 1974: 121, 129, 130) in addition to numerous advertising posters from the late nineteenth and early twentieth century. Significantly however, my informants most frequently spoke of the 1930s as the 'era' of women's bullfighting. This period which led up to the Franquist imposition of a prohibition on women performers in the mid 1930s, was dominated by a woman named Juanita Cruz, and it was also the period when Maria Gomez initiated her short career. Cruz, lauded by many as the greatest ever woman bullfighter, performed wearing a conventionally tailored traje de luces or traje corto with a skirt based on the design of the trousers. Having achieved international fame, she left Spain for Latin America once the prohibition came into force. There she graduated to matador de toros status and performed alongside top men bullfighters of her time. Until Cristina Sánchez took the alternativa in 1996 Cruz was known as the only woman to have attained this status. Aficionado conversations about her, and the numerous articles and books that commemorate her career, define the femininity represented by Juanita Cruz as appropriate to 1930s bullfighting. In one version of the discourse of tradition represented both in literature and hearsay she becomes a revered novelty. Others were of the opinion that such respect was not due, and in accordance with another strand of the narrative they severely criticised her (see Boada and Cebolla 1976: 68–190).

It seems to me that Juanita Cruz was clearly working a particular strategy of visual self-representation which won some approval from her public. She adds comment to her clothing with an expression of her own commitment: 'I remember . . . my first performance with picadores with my *cuadrilla* in Granada, the 5 May 1935, dressed in a traje de luces, in my own style, substituting the trousers for a skirt-trouser, which by feminising my clothing reflected my concept of the seriousness and responsibility of what I was doing' (quoted in Boada and Cebolla 1976: 177). Sixty years later in Córdoba, Cristina Sánchez stressed that for her début con picadores she had dressed in a *traje de luces* made by the same tailor as those of her male contemporaries and not at all at variance with the conventional design. Thus, by making her costume consistent with her commitment to following the same career path as any bullfighter, she represented it as a mark of her seriousness and desire to play by the same rules as men performers. Nevertheless, these women's statements about their clothing should not be taken to represent the meanings of their costumes. Both ritual costume and fashion garments and the bodies they are wrapped around will be made meaningful in terms of other subjectivities.

## The Trouble with Trousers . . .

In academic circles I have sometimes been asked to elaborate on the significance of a very feminine costume such as the traje de luces being worn by men bullfighters. The question, based on an assumption that the traje de luces is essentially feminine ignores the need to consider when and how it may become a gendered symbol. Marvin similarly attributes the traje with 'apparent connotations of femininity or at least non-masculinity' – it is a fabric and form of identifiable masculine and feminine elements, the latter contained in its colour, embroidery, style, etc. He argues that when this costume is worn by a woman its feminine elements are stressed; and that this creates a series of ambiguities in relation to the masculine role of the 'superman' bullfighter and results in problems of classification for men spectators. Similarly problematic for the woman performer, according to Marvin is the 'male' element of the costume; writing in the 1980s he argues that the 'traditionally male' trousers of the traje render it inappropriate for women (1988: 152). This reference to tradition does not, however, support a generalisation about why women bullfighters should not wear tight trousers – whilst aficionados may define trousers as 'traditionally male' (or possibly masculine) it does not necessarily follow that they will object to them being worn by a female performer. Furthermore, although one may regard trousers as *traditionally* masculine, one may also consider them as *currently* no more masculine than feminine. It may be true that, as Marvin notes, in the 1980s women tended to wear trousers only on informal occasions. However, during my fieldwork I observed that women wore trousers or leggings for work, formal receptions and presentations, weddings, and to the bullfight – an event which, as I point out in Chapter 3, many women dress up for.

Despite this, the argument that women should not be permitted to perform wearing a traje de luces was still evident amongst some aficionados in the 1990s. It was often linked to the analogous idea that only the real (male) bullfighter can don the traje and that women ought not imitate men bullfighters. Trivialising descriptions

**Figure 19:** The French *rejoneadora* Maria Sara maintains a place amongst the top *rejoneadores*. However, as a horseback bullfighter her status is rather different to that of women who perform on foot: the *rejoneo* is considered by many to be a more feminine activity and thus to be suitable for women to perform in as well as being more to the taste of women spectators.
© Sarah Pink

of women bullfighters as 'dressed up' in the traje de luces, associated them with women *artistes* (singers, dancers) who dressed torero style for publicity shots. In terms of the discourse about tradition this standpoint defines tradition as a guardian of gender role segregation and calls for the maintenance of this distinction in performance. Thus it was in the name of tradition that its proponents justified their rejection of the women performers in mainstream bullfighting, but as I have already indicated tradition is defined and employed in multiple ways and it seems significant that today's women performers conform to tradition by dressing in the same costumes as men. Antoñita wore either her traje de luces or traje corto according to the traditional conventions of a mainstream performance as did all of the women who I saw performing or in photographs in the 1990s (for example, Cristina Sánchez, Yolanda Carvajal, Mari-Paz Vega, Angela de los Angeles). The visual dimension of their self-representation can be interpreted to make some important distinctions, firstly, it implies sameness between themselves and their male contemporaries – all bullfighters, regardless of their biological sex, wear suits of lights and there is nothing novel, feminine, or different about a woman's traje de luces except, of course, that it is made to fit a female body. Secondly, it expresses difference from the category of woman bullfighter which was established by Juanita Cruz in the 1930s, and thus locates contemporary performers in a 'tradition of bullfighting', not a separate 'tradition of women's bullfighting'. Finally, it distinguishes them from rejoneadoras who never wear suits of lights – this is significant because the rejoneo is often classed as a more feminine type of bullfighting. Cristina Sánchez and her contemporaries use costume in a particular way to situate themselves in relation to mainstream bullfighting. Whilst women bullfighters of the 1970s and some earlier women performers also wore *trajes* with trousers their outfits were interpreted in ways specific to these historical contexts. It is not the material costume itself that is always most significant, but the ways in which it is made meaningful by different standpoints and in different historical periods.

## (More) Sexual Aspects of the Bullfight

'She's got a nice bum,' tended to be a normal, although usually isolated cry during Cristina Sánchez's early performances which I attended in 1992 to 1994. These comments would seem to support

Marvin's analysis, 'Whereas the tightness of the trousers around a male performer's body is not commented on by members of the public, the tightness around the groin and buttocks of the female performer is; the costume becomes the focus of erotic interest and the performer an object of sexual rather than artistic interest' (1988: 153). According to this version of traditionalist aficionado discourse a woman bullfighter's body is eroticised by her costume. Although Marvin's interpretation is valid for a particular standpoint, the discourse he identifies is only one amongst many others. I propose to contextualise that particular perspective on the sexuality of women bullfighters by acknowledging other ways of viewing performers' sexualities. Aficionados who speak of a woman bull-fighter's artistic worth may also view her with sexual interest, gay aficionados may find a man's performance equally erotic but similarly be able to articulate it in terms of either a narrative of performance or sexuality. Aficionadas may speak of male bull-fighters' performances in terms of their artistic value because this is an appropriate way to speak of them, whilst simultaneously appreci-ating the erotic imagery of their tight clothing. People tend to know when they should speak in particular ways about a bullfighter's performance, and this will depend on how they wish to situate and express (in this case) either their afición or their sexuality. Thus the performance of a woman wearing tight trousers is not simply either the focus of sexual or artistic interest, rather it is potentially a site for many interests and perspectives.

## Ambiguously Fashionable

The gender ambiguity of women performers in the 1930s (and also later in the 1970s) must be understood in its historical context. In the 1990s when a woman appears dressed to perform in her traje de luces she presents herself in terms of visual metaphors that may be referred to both the visual history of bullfighting and a contem-porary visual culture. Both, whilst rather different, are relevant for interpreting the ways in which she is received. Below I explore the relationship between 'ritual costume' – the traje de luces that has changed little since the mid-nineteenth century (cf. Pitt-Rivers 1990) and the constantly changing styles of modern fashion. It has been argued that the latter '*plays* endlessly with the distinction between masculinity and femininity' and is used to express 'our *shifting* ideas about . . . masculinity and femininity' (Wilson 1985: 122).

Fashion clothing goes 'out of fashion' and becomes 'ugly' or 'tasteless' in retrospect (Coward 1984: 34). In contrast, the revered traje de luces exhibits a continuity of style from season to season. Ugliness, tastelessness or impropriety are not related to the costume itself (at least by aficionados), but are only perceived when it is worn by particular bodies. An increasing number of people find it appropriate that a physically fit female body should wear a traje de luces. Moreover, overweight men may be ridiculed when they don the tight trousers of the torero. As my elderly aficionado informants pointed out, there is nothing remarkable about a woman dressing 'torero style'. For some informants this perspective applied to both inside and outside the arena: to both the ritual context and everyday life.

In a sense the interplay between the traje de luces and women's fashion superficially appears to be a one-way exchange: fashion imitates and plays with torero style and does so most explicitly in fashion photography. For example, in recent years several fashion features in *Elle*, *Marie Clare* and *Vogue* have developed this theme. Also comparable to the style of the traje de luces are the tight leggings and short jackets that women wore in the early 1990s (and continue to wear to a lesser extent in the latter half of this decade). In terms of sport, and returning to my informant's analogy to horse-riding, in the 1990s women ride in tight-fitting jodhpurs. Thus, the relation set up between women's riding and bullfighting costume for the 1930s may also be applied in the 1990s. Similarly, images of sportswomen wearing tight-fitting clothing are common-place. Whilst the traje de luces does not appear to appropriate elements of fashion clothing, attitudes to bullfighting costumes are affected by people's understandings of other sets of images that form part of their visual culture. Not surprisingly, some informants thought it both 'logical' and acceptable that a woman should perform in a traje de luces.

## Popular Culture, the Torero Youth and the Commodification of Tradition

Above I have argued that there is a significant interface between bullfight imagery and popular fashion. This may be understood in terms of the commodification of tradition. Pérez Molina (1991) describes how during the 1980s a torero style was manifested in Spanish youth culture through for example, Almodovar's feature film *Matador*, the popular music group *Toreros Muertos* (Dead Bull-fighters) and a presence of bullfighting themes in rock music and lyrics. The traje de luces, traditional settings, and torero postures have featured on record covers. Simultaneously youth fashion adopted certain facets of the traje de luces. This point was also made by several women who told me that a short cropped jacket called a torera,[5] reminiscent in shape to that of the traje de luces, had been very fashionable in the 1980s. I found that the term torera was still used to refer to women's cropped jackets. Pérez Molina interprets the 'ambiguous look' cultivated by 'smooth-faced and childlike teenagers with short hair and a *coleta* [the small plait grown by the bullfighter], lithe, agile bodies' as being related to the torero 'look' (1991: 447). I suggest that this 'ambiguous look' may also have been related to the 1980s international pop–music scene. I recognise that it would be a mistake to read too much into similarities between the iconography of bullfighting imagery and popular youth culture. Nevertheless, there appear to be some significant examples of how tradition is referenced and redefined in popular culture. References to bullfighters and bullfighting pop-music lyrics indicate that the appropriation of traditional flamenco and Spanish song has been employed as a commercial strategy. Traditional and popular culture are often pitched against one another in everyday discourse and in anthropology. For example, Marvin insists that the gender impli-cations of the traje de luces can be understood only in the ritual context. According to Marvin's analysis it is the ritual context of the bullfight that 'controls any ambiguous response to or interpretation of the traje de luces' as a feminine costume worn by a 'superman' (1988: 152). In this interpretation, the female bullfighter upsets the balance of the ritual by stressing the femininity of the costume. For traditionalist aficionado discourse this model stands, but I propose that this discourse should not be isolated, and in a wider context, Marvin's interpretation is foiled by many aficionado's positive reactions to seeing a woman in a traje de luces.[6] The relationship between the ritual performance and a broader consumer culture is crucial. I would argue that understandings of the ritual narrative cannot remain unaffected by the wider culture of which it is a part. In the case of costume the meanings invested in clothing outside of this ritual context bear significantly on the ways in which different members of the audience interpret the meaning of ritual costume. People do not think just one way about the bullfight, rather they may think about it in terms a range of different discourses which

can never be entirely separated from one another. Thus, I propose
that any discussion of the ways aficionados of any age or gender
interpret a woman wearing a traje de luces must consider the
interface between these subjectivities.

## What's in a Name? Torero or Torera

In a way analogous to their insistence that men and women
bullfighters should wear different costumes, some informants
demanded that sexual difference should also be reflected in the
gender of their title. *Torero* is the usual term for a male bullfighter.
*Matador* translates as 'killer' (not as 'bullfighter') so it refers only to
the *matador de toros*. The correct term for any performer who has
not yet taken the alternativa is not torero, but novillero, and during
my fieldwork before 1996 this was the category into which all
women bullfighters fell. These categories are respected in advertising
and reports, but in conversation the term torero is often employed
indiscriminately, unless it is used to distinguish between the novillero and torero stages of a performer's career.

Women's employment in those professions which were previously
occupied exclusively by men has presented some ambiguities for
gendered job-titles. The relationship between the gender of professional titles and the biological sex of the person undertaking the
position is uneven and inconsistent. For example, some informants
were baffled as to whether they should be calling a woman doctor
*medico* or *medica*, or the postwoman *cartero* or *cartera* – the latter
also means 'wallet'. Nevertheless, it was generally[7] assumed that the
*cartera/cartero* or *abogada/abogado* (lawyer) were engaged in the same
profession regardless of biological sex. The case for bullfighters is
less clear-cut. The feminised versions of bullfighting terms are torera
and novillera (*matadora* is less used).[8] The application of these titles
and their masculine counterparts in conversation and written
accounts is inconsistent but during my fieldwork meanings were
openly stated and negotiated and it appeared that some consensus
existed. Until recently all woman bullfighters were referred to as
toreras, those of the early twentieth century were called *Las Señoritas
Toreras*, yet in Córdoba, Cristina Sánchez firmly asserted her
objection to these terminologies.

> In the arena we are all toreros and I am the first to demand that I should
> not be called torera because of the way in which it differentiates
> between whether you are a man or a woman. In the bullring I am
> another torero whilst out of the ring I am super-feminine. And I say

very clear and loud that last year a *matador de toros* said something to me which has stayed imprinted in my mind: 'To begin with you were a woman, I watched to see what you do, but there was a moment in which you became neither man nor woman, you were a torero.'

The bullfighter had clearly said just what Cristina wanted to hear. Some aficionados, television commentators, journalists and critics take this plea seriously and refer to her as a torero or novillero. Most informants' initial reaction however was to call her *torera*. This terminology was often applied with 'good intentions'. For instance, when I attended one of her 1992 performances in Malaga, Cristina was carried out of the arena on the shoulders of a crowd chanting *torera! torera!* in recognition of her triumph. At the same time many people seemed aware that there was a question concerning her title. In 1993 I referred to this linguistic issue in a newspaper article (in *La Tribuna*, Córdoba) that I entitled 'La Mujer en el Toreo: reflecciones sobre el éxito de una mujer novillero en la temporada de '93' ('Women in bullfighting: reflections on the success of a woman bullfighter in the season of '93'). The editor seized on the torera/torero distinction and headed the article 'A woman who wants them to call her torero' (see Pink 1993a).[9]

## Toreros and Toreras in (his)tory

Historically the torero/torera distinction was significant, the toreras were in a class apart from their male contemporaries. They often performed in separate events and formed their own cuadrillas. The performance offered by the toreras was considered to be quite distinct to what occurred when men held the stage. Women's bullfighting was, in short, a feminine activity, and wholly separate from masculine activities. Whilst women performers often took part in events with novice and comic bullfighters, they rarely shared the ring with professional bullfighters. However, it was not unanimously believed that women could not cross into the torero category, for example, De Aricha, conceding to Juanita Cruz an exceptional status, used the linguistic distinction to stress his point.

> Juanita Cruz was not a señorita torera, like so many of those that are registered in the history of bullfighting. She was a torero with all the responsibility which is coupled with such a dangerous profession. (quoted in Boada and Cebolla 1976: 170)

In historical terms the torero/torera distinction was not simply a matter of biological difference for all critics. Similarly in the 1990s, some informants reasoned that a woman torero had never existed because rather than taking the alternativa and graduating to torero status in Spain, women had only attained to the novillero stage. The torero/torera categories are still a site of debate in contemporary culture: the question of whether a woman can be a torero is by no means settled.

## Right Category, Wrong Country

Whilst Juanita Cruz was labelled 'exceptional' and honoured by some with the title torero, she had no significant impact on the history of men's bullfighting. Her career, which flourished in the 1930s, was outstanding but short. Women's bullfighting, curtailed by the onset of the Spanish Civil War, was prohibited in the mid 1930s until 1974. Juanita Cruz, marginalised from her profession, could only continue performing in South America. The torero role thus developed as a uniquely masculine performance, the figures (such as Manolete and Belmonte) invoked by aficionados and historians to mark twentieth-century styles and innovations in bullfighting are all men.

As a result of the campaign of Angela Hernández (Boada and Cebolla 1976: 249–70), the prohibition was lifted in 1974. When women re-entered bullfighting the nature of performance which had been established in the rule-books, and developed exclusively by and for male performers, was dominated by a strong masculine identity. In 1990, Maribel Atienza and Angela Hernández, the women bullfighters of the 1970s, were referred to as Señoritas Toreras with the conviction that 'el toreo es cosa de hombres' (the bullfight is a thing for men) (Ladis 1991: 85–7). Marvin points out that Maribel Atienza strove to maintain a feminine image in her bullfighting style, so as not to appear to be attempting to copy men bullfighters (1988: 164). Maribel was a novillera, she did not classify or represent herself as a novillero, nor did she aspire to be a torero. The feminised performance of Maribel stated her gender unambiguously.

## Male and Female Toreros of the 1990s

In the 1990s the situation is more complex because women and men are both claiming to be toreros regardless of their biological sex. The strong masculine identity of the bullfighter figure is problematic for women toreros because it implies an ambiguous gender identity that some people find disturbing. Others, however, take this ambiguity for granted. Moreover, given that according to some theorists ambiguity is fashionable in popular culture (see below), it may sometimes even be considered appropriate.

The career structures and both long- and short-term aspirations of contemporary women bullfighters are much more closely matched with those of their male counterparts than with those of the señoritas toreras of the past. They aspire to perform in professional events, and participate with their male contemporaries in the lottery by which each performer is allotted two bulls on a random basis (unlike rejoneadores who are usually separately allocated more appropriate bulls with shaved horns). Some men oppose the incorporation of women into mainstream bullfighting and in 1993 several leading novilleros refused to perform with Cristina Sánchez. Subsequent to Pedrito de Portugal's publicised rejection of a contract to perform with Cristina, it was announced that she would undertake a single-handed performance to kill all six bulls herself. Some informants complimented Cristina's bravery. Not only did she defy her competitor's scorn, but two hours of continuous performance with six bulls is a tiring and difficult feat, which was taken by some informants as evidence that Cristina was more than worthy of sharing the ring with a man performer. In general, aficionado opinion over whether or not women and men should perform alongside one another is divided. Some suggested that it would be more appropriate for women to perform in separate 'women's bullfights' in a comparison of the situation to women's tennis or athletics. Others insisted that Pedrito de Portugal should be forced to perform with Cristina Sánchez. Several informants accused him of cowardice and one man proposed that his refusal was owing to his fear that Cristina would show him up. This informant (a locally respected aficionado) suggested the novillero should face up to the challenge of recognising that Cristina was a talented performer and in every way his equal.

Several live bullfights featuring women performers only were broadcast on television during my fieldwork. I noticed that these events have been feminised by certain discourses. For example, in 1993 *Aplausos* announced one such performance as a 'superfeminine bullfight'. The novelty status of 'all women' events is in a sense rooted in the idea of a historical tradition of señoritas toreras. As such these performances become marketable curiosities, potentially useful for television ratings and live ticket-sales. Some would argue that 'true aficionados' would neither reach into their pockets nor pick up their television's remote control in honour of such an event. However, these performances appeared to be successful and many of my informants had at least taken the trouble to view part of the televised performances. At the beginning of their careers, women bullfighters may have to sacrifice their ambition in order to be integrated directly into mainstream bullfighting. By performing in these 'feminised' bullfights they at least have an opportunity to perform in recognised arenas and their successes must be counted in the league tables.

A polar distinction between las señoritas toreras and *una mujer torero* thus differentiates between female, feminine bullfighters who perform a feminised bullfight, and mainstream bullfighters who are of female sex. The second category contains contradictory terminology, and in that sense it questions an essentialist gender dichotomy. The term mujer torero is becoming more commonly used both in conversation and in the media. Nevertheless, a name alone does not indicate that women's performances are not feminised in discourse or interpretation. The feminisation of a performance occurs in different ways at different stages of the communication process and may be initiated, experienced or imposed by a whole variety of individuals. For example, the bullfighter herself, the television commentator, informal spectator commentaries, other personal subjective interpretations, may all contribute to the extent of a performance's feminisation. I would therefore argue that whether or not a performance is feminised thus depends on the subject position of the individual who interprets what he or she sees.

### Fashionably Ambiguous?

Epstein and Straub locate gender ambiguity at the forefront of popular culture and suggest that it is pitched against essentialist identity and right-wing conservatism, thereby proposing that gender ambiguity may offer liberation from identity (1991: 9). This approach offers an interesting political perspective on the gender ambiguity perceived in the role of women bullfighters, but simultaneously locates women bullfighters in a double bind as regards conservatism. The women bullfighters of the 1990s are conservative in that they wish to perform the traditional mainstream bullfight and will admit no changes in the performance rules or structure. But they simultaneously challenge the gendered role to which traditional convention allocates them. If popular culture is viewed as a domain in which such transgressions and the overturning of tradition (in its own name) are fashionable it can be argued that popular culture has a part in the wider cultural context in which women have become more popular as performers. Similarly, a recent retelling of a (true?) story set in the early twentieth century may be interpreted as having an analogous political edge and has been voiced as the tale of a woman achiever. During my fieldwork I read (in Boada and Cebolla 1976: 133–6, and Rivas 1990: 294–7) and was told, the story of La Reverte several times. The tale of this performer features in most accounts of the history of women's bullfighting and was woven into several discussions. As the story is told by Rivas, and Boada and Cebolla it does little to support the historical tradition argument. La Reverte, a biological male, disguised himself as a woman to pursue a very successful career as a *señorita torera* in the early twentieth century. However, when the first prohibition was placed on women bullfighters in 1908 he revealed his true sexual identity and began to perform as a man. Unfortunately, on the male circuit his skills, that had been well respected in a woman, did not come up to scratch. Shortly afterwards he retired to work as a guard on a ganadería. One of the accounts I came across included a photograph of the late middle-aged, rather plump La Reverte. An interpretation of this tale is that women can only bullfight when they are really men, and any failed bullfighter could succeed if he disguised himself as a woman. The tale also lends a sense of the carnivalesque to women's bullfighting and it affirms links between women performers and comic bullfighters. But Feiner (1995: 96–9) plays a trump card by revealing after still more research that La Reverte was biologically female. She claims that the woman had grown up on a ganadería, and that she was an ardent aficionada who performed as a woman until the 1908 prohibition when, in order to be able to continue her career, she disguised herself as a man. This version thus transforms the story into one of a woman with a powerful and dedicated afición. Thus Feiner switches the narrative from one in which a man achieved fame through an exploitation of women's bullfighting, to tell of a woman's strategy for being faithful to her vocation. In the 1990s this new tale of La Reverte becomes a story of a woman who disguised her sex and in doing so challenged conservatism. Moreover, in describing her ambiguous gender in this way Feiner sets La Reverte in opposition to another narrative that I encountered in the commentaries of aficionados, fiction and documentary sources. The question of whether women ever worked in direct physical contact with the bulls was straightforward: ganaderos said that they had never employed women in their establishments, nor had it occurred to them to do so. Instead I was told that at most the wife and daughters of the live-in workers may ride over the land with the manager whilst he was checked on the animals. A development of this scenario is represented in the 'true story' of the bull *Civilón* in the 1930s, and in Horcajada García's (1968) novel *Soñador*. Both texts portray the relationship between the daughters of the manager and a particularly noble bull. In these tales the bull, responding to the 'feminine touch' of these women, becomes a pet that they stroke and caress. The bull's nobility is manifested in his pledge never to harm them and later in his outstanding performance in the arena which result in his being granted his life and a return to the ganadería (for *Civilón* however the happy ending was short lived: he is reported to have been slaughtered for meat during the shortages of the civil war).

When the gender of contemporary women bullfighters is rendered ambiguous it distinguishes them from a feminised historical tradition of women's bullfighting. When toreras are given their own feminine history, costume and name they pose no threat to malestream bullfighting. In contrast, those who step into the mainstream arena wearing a suit of lights and calling themselves toreros claim a stake in a history to which they present a difficult challenge.

## The History of Women in Bullfighting

The supposed historical tradition of toreras pertains to a more general history of women in bullfighting. The woman spectator also has a history. An analysis of the iconography of art and photography that represents women at bullfights implies a construction of historical continuity that lends the model a traditional-historical justification (see Chapter 3). Ganaderas are also associated with a tradition in which women have been given or inherited ganaderías. Some other feminine roles are excluded from the history of bullfighting, for example, photographers, journalists, managers and business women (see Chapter 4). In comparison with the ganadera and spectator, the roles of women bullfighting photographers and journalists are not justified by a historical tradition within bullfight culture. Rather their acceptability appears to be related to the contemporary context where professional photography and journalism are considered appropriate activities for women. Moreover, as photographers and journalists women appear not to pose a direct threat to the traditional bullfight.

## Names, Clothes and Bodies

One of the central themes of this chapter is an exploration of the ways in which people classify women performers within their own particular visions of the world, its history and in particular its gender relations. Decisions about the name used to refer to a woman performer, or interpretations of the costume in which she performs are inevitably bound up with knowledge and ideas which are not usually related to the bullfight. In this sense neither the ritual context not the historical evolution of gender roles in bullfighting exist in isolation from wider cultural narratives and discourses. In the next chapter the focus turns to the body itself in order to explore how different understandings and experiences of the performing woman's body are articulated.

# Notes

1. Some of the ideas developed in this section were first introduced in an article published in Córdoba during my fieldwork (Pink 1994).

2. La Pajulera was active in the 1770s and is best known from Goya's etchings in which she is represented on horseback (see Boada and Cebolla 1976: 35–7).

3. These texts represent the most complete attempts to document the history of women in bullfighting. They are both written from a standpoint that states the need to uncover women's historical participation in bullfighting and to recognise the battle women have fought to secure a place in that world.

4. Image produced by Gonzalez, reproduced by Boada and Cebolla (1976: 116).

5. The full label is *chaqueta torera* (bullfighting/bullfighter jacket). Shortened to *torera* the adjective takes the feminine form from the feminine *chaqueta*.

6. Sociologists of clothing have argued that some of the ambivalences surrounding women's entry into professional careers and business are

represented in clothing, and that women have 'more rights to play with sartorial gender signs that men do' (Corrigan 1992: 152).
7. However, I did once heard the argument that women lawyers should take 'softer' cases.
8. *Matadora* is used more in American English literature and biography, for example, Fifield's (1960) novel *Matadora* and Verill Cintrón's (1960) biography of Conchita Cintrón.
9. Informants were aware of the linguistic issues before I published this article.

# seven

# Breasts in the Bullring: Female Physiology, Women Bullfighters and Competing Femininities[1]

'**S**he was the pure bullfight represented in the body of a woman,' ex-bullfighter Domingo Ortega is reputed to have said of Juanita Cruz. His words, intended as a compliment of the highest form to the woman in question, also invoke the supposed incongruity of combining the female body and the bullfight.

### Performing Bodies

In my conversations about women bullfighters with both aficionados and those who were little concerned about bullfighting, the body was a frequent focus. In particular, men's and women's comparative physiologies and strengths were cited to justify claims that women were unsuited to bullfighting. The body is similarly present in other accounts. For instance, Grosso represents a common notion that the bullfight is an embodied experience for both performers and audience. He writes that the performance is concerned with bodily sensations that can only be felt through experience – they cannot be evoked by verbal or written description, photography or film (1992: 20–1). In anthropological work the body has been represented as central both to the performance and Andalusian understandings of the bullfight (Corbin and Corbin 1986: 110; Marvin 1988: 163). In this chapter I shall focus on the centrality of the human body to different standpoints on women performers by considering how a heterogeneous audience (Finnegan 1992: 99–100) responds to and classifies a female bullfighting body. My analysis of this issue will encompass two related themes. Firstly

I shall explore how different perspectives on femininity make a female body meaningful in relation to the embodied experience of a traditional feminine lifecycle model; and secondly how different subjectivities treat the expression of the embodied experience of bullfighting through a female body. From different standpoints the latter may appear perfectly appropriate or utterly problematic and I will relate these contrasting perspectives to wider debates and issues concerning gender and the body both in anthropology and in Andalusian culture. Whilst women bullfighters themselves do not constitute a political movement, their actions can be related to political debates and the issue of the status of women in Spain.

## Bullfighting through the Lifecycle

In Chapter 2 I introduced the idea that if the bullfight is to be viewed as drama then the mixed-sex bullfight may be interpreted as telling a range of different stories about men and women in Spanish culture. If gendered experience is taken to be embodied, the body inevitably enters into these stories. Thus, to a certain extent the female performing body can be interpreted as a statement about ways of using and experiencing the female body. The details of women's lifecycles in contemporary Spain are diverse and varied; there is no single model for the 'successful woman' and the body projects of different women are tailored to meet plural ends. A woman bullfighter thus treats and experiences her body quite differently to a woman committed to childbearing and motherhood. For this analysis, differences amongst women are particularly significant and it is important to recognise a diversity of models and experiences of women's lifecycles, rather than just one model. For example, a common version of a traditional feminine lifecycle model assumes: the quest for a boyfriend before marriage, engagement, marriage, motherhood, caring for one's children, husband, and ageing parents, and becoming a grandmother. Many women may speak of their own and other women's experiences in terms of this model, yet it should not be taken for granted that women who follow or refer to this sequence do so in the same way or have the same experiences. Some informants used these lifecycle stages as points of reference when discussing women bullfighters. For example, some proposed that women bullfighters have relatively short careers spanning from their mid-twenties until marriage and childbearing in their late-twenties. These ideas were articulated in

1992 when the ex-bullfighter, Angela Hernández, publicised her intention to make a comeback. Some informants, following a traditional feminine lifecycle narrative criticised Angela, proposing that she was too old to bullfight and observing that since she had failed when she was young (at the appropriate point in her lifecycle) it was doubtful that she would succeed in middleage. Whilst her opponents claimed that Angela was trying to cash in on Cristina's success, Angela articulated a rather different narrative of historical change by stressing that the 1990s may offer her an opportunity to participate in fair competition.

## 'Communicative Bodies'

In Chapter 2 I introduced a distinction between representation and presentation whereby the performance represents a bullfighter's public success but simultaneously entails a presentation of his/her embodied art and knowledge. Male and female bullfighters' bodies are usually made meaningful in terms of different narratives and whilst the presentation involves a recognisable format of visual play (and display), the male body is exchanged for a female body. This invokes questions of how such an exchange affects the rendering and interpretation of the performing body and the skills it presents. If one accepts Frank's idea of the 'communicative body', this will entail asking about 'the capacity for recognition which is enhanced through the sharing of narratives which are fully embodied,' and recognising that, 'What is shared is one body's sense of another's experience' (1991: 89). It seems appropriate to apply this idea to bullfighting about which it is said that an enhanced understanding derives from having performed or at least practised the cape passes; thus the informed spectator is able to identify with the bodily experience of the bullfighter. Such an idea suggests two ways in which women performers may be problematic for a traditionalist aficionado: first, he may refuse to identify a female body as a bullfighter's body; and second by not identifying his own body with the performing female body he would not imagine that body's 'sense of experience'. This offers one (but not the only) way of under-standing how some of the standpoints represented below may not enable spectators to share the embodied narrative of the bullfight represented by a female body.

Similarly, when a viewer takes the bullfighter's body to stand for the gendered life-experience of a sexed body a binary distinction leaves no place for women performers. If a bullfighter's success is situated in the lifecycle of a male body and if it entails the public demonstration of a physical peak of fitness (rather than a female body lifecycle associated with childbirth, menstruation, menopause), the female bullfighter's body lifecycle (thus interpreted as following a different pattern) cannot fit into the life-plan of a bullfighting career.

## The Flesh of the Debate

So called 'practical' objections to women bullfighters tend to refer to male/female physiological, psychological or simply 'natural' differences and they usually reflect the ideas of traditional discourse. Whilst some informants attributed unequal male and female ability, achievement, and behaviour to biology or 'nature', others saw difference as culturally determined. I shall begin by discussing some of the discourses on physiology which emerge from the conversation and literature of the bullfighting world. However, most of the traditional standpoints that I represent below are unacceptable to many Andalusians in the 1990s; and moreover, some dominant contemporary images of the female body deviate from traditionalist models. Particularly challenging are the 'new radicalized images of female physicality' that emerged with the female sporting body-image. These feminine images show 'some collapse of conventional points of reference, some acceptance of values which have previously been marginalized' (Hargreaves 1994: 173) – they represent a femininity compatible with some women's desire to perform the bullfight with their female bodies. The interplay between bullfight culture and other aspects of culture is significant if one is to understand how women performers are situated. For example, in a 1990s magazine interview, the sporting body is drawn into the equation in a photograph of Cristina Sánchez sitting in sports training clothes with a cape beside her.[2]

## Breasts in the Bullring

In traditionalist discourse there has been a curious emphasis on the incompatibility of breasts with bullfighting. The 'practical problem' of the position of breasts, is thought to prevent women from making the movements appropriate to bullfighting. This, and the concern that breasts are excessively vulnerable to injury are denied by women performers who confirm that their breasts present no physical problem as regards following exactly the same bullfighting procedure as their male contemporaries. The 'breast problem' owes more to traditionalist masculine understandings of the social and biological functions of breasts than to women bullfighters' experiences of their own bodies.

The 'breast problem' is explicit in public bullfighting discourse. In March 1993 the woman bullfighter Cristina Sánchez gave a talk followed by a question and answer session to a mixed-sex audience in Córdoba's bullfighting museum. An elderly man volunteered the breast issue:

Cristina, I'm going to ask you a rather insolent question, but until now no woman, as far as I know, when she adorns herself by dressing for the bullfight . . . for example, the breast is the part of the woman's body which is most sensitive and because they can so easily be subjected to being knocked, do you wear any kind of special protection?

Cristina's answer was more composed than the embarrassed curiosity behind the question. 'The men don't wear anything "there", she said, pointing towards her groin, and the audience clapped their approval, not only of her retort to what had indeed been an insolent question but also her calm and down-to-earth approach to an otherwise delicate situation. 'My clothing is the same as that of any man, isn't it? I dress myself at a tailors . . . Of course for men it's worse, they have it "'there'",' she continued to further applause. She had aptly provided a denial of the model of femininity which was implicit in the question.

The elderly man's question reflected general curiosity, but the comment of the young men and women with whom I spoke later revealed how some thought it inappropriate and ridiculous. In a local newspaper article (*La Tribuna* 7 November 1993) the Cordoban writer Maña makes similar objections to women bullfighters. His argument focuses not on women's failure to perform successfully, but on the inappropriate presence of breasts and vaginas in the bullring. In the first paragraph the writer strips the bullfighter of her clothes, and he simultaneously denies and displays what several women informants in their mid-twenties to thirties classified as a 'paternalistic sexism' which asserts that women must be protected from themselves. Maña writes:

Let it be clear that I do not begin from any sexist premise – I love them too much not to give way to their whims and fancies – but however hard I try, I can't see such sweet, succulent and upright breasts amongst [the] embroidered adornments [of the bullfighters clothing].

The vulnerability of breasts is a common theme. Injury to any bullfighter is most imminent when he/she leans over the horns to kill by thrusting the sword between the bull's shoulder-blades. Some male informants assumed that the location of a woman's breasts would impede the perfection of this movement. The kill is the most dangerous action in the repertoire of the male bullfighter, and one could argue that concern for her breasts is closely related to the notion that a woman should not be publicly exposed to danger.

Discussions of breast injuries revealed the traditionalist assumption that medical treatment of such an injury may somehow be 'different from usual', or that surgery may be more complicated than it would be for a 'normal' (man's) wound. It was suggested by one informant that doctors have no 'special' ways of dealing with a ruptured breast because specialists have developed ways of attending cornadas (horn wounds) for a 'male' physiology. This belief is voiced in terms of a medical concern and scientific problem (cf. Boada and Cebolla 1976: 362). I asked some university-educated men and women in their twenties to respond to this attitude; their counter-argument was that a breast cornada is as treatable as any other damaged tissue.

The stress on the dangers of breast wounds is explained partly by cultural discourses which proclaim the primary purpose of the breast to be for motherhood – the vocation of a 'complete'[3] woman. Those who consider the risk to a breast to be too great to justify women's performances do not usually regard the possible destruction of the male genitals as equally problematic. Serious genital injuries could prevent a bullfighter from ever fathering a child; in contrast, damage to a breast need not impede pregnancy. The concern over breasts expresses a model of the 'proper' roles for two different classes of people – those with breasts and those without breasts – and it constructs fixed gender identities on the basis of biological difference. The visual comparison of the bodies of male and female performers centres on the breasts as symbols of biological sex and social role.

## Vaginas in Dangerous Places

In the newspaper article quoted above Maña goes on to refer to a Cordoban bullfighting anecdote. The Spanish word *conejo* translates as 'rabbit', but also means 'vagina'. During the nineteenth century a Cordoban bullfighter nicknamed *Conejito* (little rabbit) on one occasion fought alongside a woman bullfighter. The woman suffered minor injuries which were reported in a telegram which concluded that 'the *Conejito*' had remained unharmed. In Maña's text the anecdote becomes a vehicle for ridiculing the idea that a vagina should ever have been present in the bullring. This source of local amusement was cited by several male informants on different occasions, and seemed to be appreciated by many more. Two themes appeared to underlaying its frequent retelling: first, a stress on the biological or 'natural' distinction between the sexes; second, since the woman bullfighter's vagina had remained undamaged, she remained just as much a woman as before. The joke is not universally appreciated, and its repetition must be contextualised by the local practice in bullfighting circles of telling and retelling various historical bullfighting anecdotes.

## Parenting and Performance

In Andalusia there are a great variety of ideas concerning motherhood and childbirth. Many people believe that the proper role for a woman is that of wife and mother; that married women should be expected both to have children and to stay at home to care for them. In contrast whilst emphasising the importance of their own mothers as the bedrock of the home and family, many young women say that they do not intend to follow similar patterns in life. As I have discussed in Chapter 1, in recent years the issue of the working mother has become a policy and practical concern for the Instituto de la Mujer. Women's organisations participate in campaigns to help young and mature women enter the job market by running consulting sessions and skills-acquisition courses.

Although the notions of woman as child bearer and bullfighter are not totally incompatible, the lifecycle model of the former imposes certain restrictions on the career of a woman bullfighter. Women bullfighters are expected, by those who identify a woman's role as that of wife and mother, to conform to the model. It is assumed that once married a woman bullfighter will stop performing; her taurine activities are classified as a short, pre-marital occupation. The 1950s horseback performer Conchita Cintrón was often quoted by my informants and in the literature I studied as the ideal model of a woman bullfighter. She became famous for her outstanding performances but once she became engaged to be married she ended her bullfighting career (Verill Cintrón 1960). Some emphasise the fact that she had six children and thus fulfilled her 'natural' destiny as a mother (see Saez Boil) – further proof of her 'completeness'. 'Traditionalists' expect women bullfighters to marry and fulfil the feminine potential of motherhood. I met no one who considered motherhood to be compatible with the life of a bullfighter; in contrast, male bullfighters are expected to be fathers and performers simultaneously. Traditionalist aficionados blamed the wives and children of bullfighters for their declining standards of performance. When the bullfighter Espartaco, who had previously topped the league of professional bullfighting, married and became a father he began to perform less frequently. Media reports and informants' comments suggested that he had switched to a more cautious style now that he had a family. The equation between parenthood and bullfighting varied according to gender: whilst bullfighting threatens motherhood, fatherhood threatens good bullfighting. In contrast, other contemporary Andalusian discourses about female physiology, motherhood, and feminine lifecycles represent a variety of models for feminine life-plans.

## Menstruation and Bullfighting

Pitt-Rivers proposed a symbolic connection between menstruation, menstrual blood and the bullfight. His work is aptly described by Buckley and Gottleib's observation that 'the majority of ethnographic reports of menstrual customs and beliefs have been restricted to terse statements on "the" meaning of menstrual blood – seen always as symbolically dangerous or otherwise defiling' (1988: 4).

Pitt-Rivers interprets the final sword thrust which kills the bull as the violation of a menstrual taboo and a denial of male fear of female sexuality (1984: 38). He supports these speculations by citing Andalusian popular beliefs in the dangerous powers of menstruating women, for example, their ability to spoil food or put out fire by looking at it (1984: 39). Whilst certain menstrual taboos, usually limited to food preparation, are practised in southern Europe (Lawrence 1988), dominant Spanish models of menstruation reflect the scientific–medical paradigm associated with Euro-American interpretations of the body.[4] It is the compatibility of this model of menstruation with bullfighting which begs attention.

I discussed the issue of menstruation and bullfighting with over twenty young women who were all under thirty years old. The most strongly reflected opinion was that the reduced 'rationality', concentration, and physical accuracy which dominate the interpretation and experience of menstruation in the west could affect a woman bullfighter's performance. Similarly, I spoke with several non-traditionalist men of the same age-group who supported women bullfighters but who felt that the physical and emotional symptoms of menstruation may endanger them. Martin writes that, 'An overriding theme in the changes women articulate is a loss of ability to carry on activities involving mental or physical discipline' women competitive tennis players say 'their reaction times can be slower' and professional singers 'lose voice control' (Martin 1987: 121). In western capitalist society where the dominant production model values time-effectiveness and cost-effectiveness, body discipline is of paramount importance (Martin 1987: 121–2). In bullfighting, control over mind and body is fundamental; whilst a tennis player's sluggish reactions may lose her a match, a bullfighter may lose her life. In bullfighting discourse the deaths of male bullfighters are often attributed to similar losses of rationality and physical control: lack of responsibility is induced by alcohol, and drunkenness is caused by emotional pain (Conrad 1952; Insúa 1971). For one woman bullfighter at least, menstruation is also a matter of mind over body; Yolanda Caravajal has stated 'that if on the first day of menstruation, it hurts to bullfight, she quickly forgets it through force of will' (MacClancy 1996).

In order to free themselves from a perceived 'hormonal dictatorship' many Spanish women depend on medical science to administer pills in order to 'control' what is deemed 'natural'. Thus the natural state of the female body is biologically/medically identified as being in need of treatment to render the 'natural' physiological differences between the sexes irrelevant. In the case of bullfighting, uncontrolled menstruation stands for gender difference and constructs an other obstacle to women bullfighters.

The bullfight demands constant productivity of a high standard and quality. Martin suggests that menstrual cycles may inhibit women's maintenance of constant performance levels in the workplace, indicating that when their performance levels drop women may be thought to 'malfunction'. The nature of the work demanded of bullfighters values highly quality (of bulls and performances), continuity (bullfighters are expected to fight almost continuously – this signifies success) and high levels of productivity (rating is by numbers of performances and trophies). A model of continuous training and performance and constant or improving quality is clearly incompatible with a menstrual cycle throughout which the levels of one's quality of performance vary. This holds true for many professions in the public sphere; 'women find in the concrete experience of their bodies a different notion of time that counters the way time is socially organised in our industrial society' (Martin 1987: 197). It is important to remember that the bullfight was constructed by men, for men's participation, and it is based on a masculine perspective on the world.

Bullfighting (a business that depends on modern western capitalism) and the menstrual cycle represent two incompatible systems of organising time. However, the empirical evidence indicates that some women 'control' menstruation and begin careers in the profession of bullfighting.

## Minds, Bodies and Emotions

In 1993 Cristina Sánchez featured in the colour supplement of *El Mundo* newspaper.[5] The question of whether women's physical build and strength are less adapted to bullfighting than that of their male contemporaries was broached by a diagram showing Cristina's height of 1.60 metres – only 10 centimetres taller than the average bull, the caption for which read: 'Cristina's physique is a handicap with regard to the disproportionate power of the *torera* and the animal.'[5] In written and spoken debates over women's bullfighting it is frequently proposed that between the sexes there is an uneven distribution of strength, intelligence, fear, sensitivity and predictability.

## Gendered Strength and Intelligence

The arguments of most Andalusians with whom I discussed the matter were based on the premise that men are stronger than women although not necessarily more intelligent. De la Fuente reflects a common perspective when he states that it seems ridiculous to prevent women from bullfighting given that women are as successful as men in other professions (for example, government, medicine, law, engineering) which until the 1940s were exclusively male fields. He compares bullfighting to sport, where women 'recognise' that they cannot compete against men, and he interprets this as a limitation but not an implication of inferiority nor a reason why women should not compete against one another (de la Fuente 1993: 604–5). In discussion, five different all-male groups of informants of varying ages and social classes reiterated the

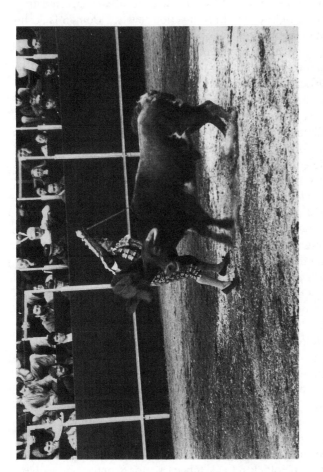

**Figure 20:** I took several photographs of Cristina Sánchez performing the kill. In some she can be seen to have successfully inserted the sword: she frequently killed quickly and smoothly. However, the image included here is of interest because it represents an occasion on which Cristina experienced some difficulty killing her bull. This type of photograph tends to be referenced as 'evidence' in arguments that women are physically or intellectually unsuited to performing the kill.
© Sarah Pink

possibility of all-women performances, or alternatively suggested that at the level when the bulls are younger, lighter and smaller, performances should be of mixed sex. Others argued that the bullfight has always had to be adapted to the physical possibilities of women performers – the 'size and the integrity of the bull is reduced' (Saez Boil nd: 89). Men and women alike suggested that whilst they may fight calves in non-serious events, women lack the strength and height to perform on foot with fully grown bulls. Most identified the problem as one of physical strength rather than intelligence, but some (men) thought women insufficiently intelligent to bullfight. Others distinguished between masculine and feminine intelligence and specialisations, concluding that women's intelligence was unsuitable for either understanding or fighting bulls.

Similar distinctions were frequently made between men's and women's physical strength. Exhibitions of feminine strength were considered appropriate whereas a woman who demonstrates masculine strength was thought 'unnatural'. Whilst women are strong enough to do housework, lift heavy objects, and to do manual labour in the fields, these activities do not challenge gender stereotypes. In contrast, one informant spoke of a young woman from his home village who was extraordinarily strong – 'as strong as any man'. He remarked that although she was 'biologically female, physically it seemed that she was almost a man'; when one saw her walking down the street it was 'as if she wasn't really a woman'. He considered it possible but not 'natural' for a woman to be strong 'like a man'. The physical strength exhibited by this particular woman had led people in the village to doubt that she were classifiable as a woman. The living proof that masculinity can be embodied in women was regarded sufficiently strange to merit comment both inside and outside the village. My informant suggested that male physical strength is an evolutionary phenomenon: over many generations, owing to an emphasis on the development of muscles and strength, men have evolved as the physically stronger sex, thus the masculine woman becomes an evolutionary and biological freak. Since Cristina Sánchez has evolved as a 'natural woman', he concluded, she will never be strong enough to perform with fully grown bulls.

The natural weakness accredited to women's arms was frequently cited by men and women aficionados as a disadvantage for women bullfighters. I was told that Maria Gomez, the Cordoban woman bullfighter of the 1930s, never performed the kill because she took seriously the belief (which a woman in her teens considered masculine and sexist) that women's arms were not strong enough to kill a bull. In the 1990s similar assertions still prevail. Cristina Sánchez's difficulties in performing the kill were often attributed to weak arms, whilst male bullfighters suffering similar problems were said simply to need to practise and develop their technique. Some informants said that women bullfighters encounter problems working with the cape owing to the weakness of their arms – capes are heavy, and strength and endurance are required to hold and accurately manipulate a cape throughout a twenty-minute performance. During the viewing of a televised performance one traditionalist claimed to see that Cristina's arms were too weak to extend the cape correctly. However, generalisation is inappropriate: ultimately people interpret the sexual distribution of strength and intelligence according to their own subject positions. For example, Antoñita strongly refuted the suggestion that women were unable to develop sufficient strength in their arms to bullfight.

### Gendered Fear

Whilst some informants classified fear as feminine, others distinguished between masculine and feminine fear. A model of irrational feminine fear was applied to women bullfighters, who were said to be 'terrified of mice but unafraid to confront a dangerous bull'. Masculine fear was referred to as 'natural'; in order to display a masculine strength of character men must overcome fear. The bullfighter is expected to experience rational fear before and in the first moments of a performance, and bullfighters will happily admit to this. Failure entails not overcoming fear whilst the triumphant hero is he who dominates both himself – his fear – and the bull. Two male ex-bullfighters and several aficionados suggested that if a woman felt such fear she would not even consider trying to bullfight because women are incapable of the bravery required to overcome masculine fear. Therefore some people will characterise aspiring women bullfighters as unaware of the 'real' danger and 'rational' fear of bullfighting. Some suggested that since the bullfight looks very easy from the point of view of the audience, women wish to try it owing to their lack of understanding and oblivion to both its danger and difficulty.

Other informants said that an awareness of danger will deter women from bullfighting. Several aficionadas told me that they would be too scared to bullfight. Similarly, in conversation some traditionalist men claimed that a woman bullfighter who had been present when a bullfighter was killed in the arena never performed again because witnessing the death of one of Spain's best bullfighters made her finally understand the reality of danger and the feeling of fear.

However, in non-traditional discourses the sex and gender of fear and bravery are reorganised. For example, the traditionalist model of masculine bravery embodied in the notion of 'testicular power' or 'courage' is realigned in some contemporary conceptualisations of the sex–gender association. Marvin (1988) and Corbin stress the importance of male physiology – of 'having balls' (Corbin 1978: 4) to the strength of character required of the bullfighter – a quality both essentially (i.e. biologically) and socially masculine. I found, in contrast, that in the 1990s it was common for Andalusians to evaluate positively a 'brave' and publicly assertive woman as 'having balls'. The woman bullfighter Cristina Sánchez herself claims to have metaphorical balls[6] and she is identified by some as both an icon of feminine beauty and a brave bullfighter. In these discourses which redefine masculinity and femininity, testicular power is not exclusive to those who have testicles. The terminology has been retained but the concept does not refer to an exclusively masculine social characteristic.

## Biological Sex, Gendered Activities and Social Inequalities

The 'naturalisation' of gender difference and subsequent 'de-naturalisation' of those who transgress the boundaries of masculinity and femininity are constant themes in the arguments against women bullfighters. They are classified as hybrid creatures with, in the words of one TV commentator, 'male minds and female bodies' and as women who don't even seem as if they are women; and these interpretations represent some of the traditionalist responses to the threat posed by non-traditional femininities. The visual display of a woman bullfighter illuminates the physiological differences between the sexes and for traditionalists this reinforces the notion of a natural and unalterable inequality between 'men' and 'women'. In this way, distinct male and female biological and social roles are naturalised and the conviction that these natural boundaries ought not to be transgressed is reinforced. One informant drew the analogy that for a woman to be a bullfighter is as unnatural as for a man to be a midwife; many feel that the desire to fight bulls is simply not 'normal' for a woman.[7] Women are supposed to have a 'natural

tendency' towards the business of life-giving (for example, mid-
wifery), rather than the life-taking and life-threatening profession
of bullfighting.

The ways in which inequality is embodied are stressed by beliefs
that the 'functions' of women's bodies render them less suitable than
men for successful professional performances. Similarly, embodied
and gendered emotions and thoughts are central to the ways in
which performers are believed to internalise, think and express
the bullfight. This is illustrated by the claim that, since feminine
intelligence does not understand bullfighting, women could not
embody the intellect required to direct their female bodies as if they
were bullfighters' bodies (i.e. male bodies). This belief that sexual
difference is coterminous with inequalities between men and
women implies fundamental equality amongst men. In bullfighting
lore this is represented by the idea that all men regardless of their
social class are born equal and will naturally find their place in the
social order: thus a bullfighter may emerge from any social class, his
success will represent his individual destiny. Wealth is thought to
reduce a bullfighter's willingness to expose himself to danger but it
is not believed to damage his 'natural' embodied bullfighting skill.

For the women performers themselves and for many of their
supporters who are able to identify with both the sensations and
emotions of the bullfight and with the success story of the bullfighter being a part of the embodied experience of being a woman,
there is nothing ominous about women's bullfighting.[8] However,
for those who set and naturalise the limits of masculinity and
femininity in more clearly segregated zones, a woman bullfighter
may be seen as a threat to the natural order, and thus she challenges
the individual's position in that order. This interpretation of a
woman as a threat is not uncommon in situations where women
perform in public domains which have previously been exclusively
male (Mansfield and McGinn 1993: 57). In the case of women
bullfighters, de-naturalisation is in some contexts resolved by a
play on the novelty element of women bullfighters; since they
are unnatural, uncommon, and novel, they tend to be classified as
curious oddities: exceptions to be marvelled at rather than revolut-
ionary or change-producing phenomena. From such a perspective
women bullfighters may be regarded as harmless. Thus the extent to
which women bullfighters are able to use their performance skills
to deconstruct traditionalist 'ideologies of the female body' (Frank
1991: 82–3) is limited.

## Bodies in Revolutionary Ritual?

I have explored body uses, body communication and embodied experience by focusing largely on aficionado's and other discourses about the female bullfighter's body. However, if we are to classify the live bullfight as ritual and also concede that the female bullfighter's live performance is ritual (rather than spectacle), it is useful to consider the kind of ritual process her body is involved in. This invokes the question of how feminine life drama and new feminine body-images in the bullfight can be reconciled with the idea of ritual as *rite de passage*.

Parkin treats the body and body–mind relationship as central to ritual and extends his 'spatial idea of ritual to the body itself' by referring to both physical and metaphorical bodily movement (1992: 22). I have argued that a woman's performance represents a state-ment about female body-use and body-image. The performance may be seen as a ritual statement about these notions of the female body through which it is relocated in a new position in society and culture – both physically in the bullring and metaphorically. The new body use symbolises a new body–relationship to the rest of the society by which the female body stands for not a reproducing body, but a publicly proven, physically fit body, and a successful, 'dominating' body.

Parkin goes on to emphasise that in ritual the inseparability of body and mind is stressed (1992: 23). This is an important theme in the bullfight. A woman bullfighter who uses a 'reproducing body' and a 'feminine mind' for male action, oversteps the boundaries set by conventional bullfighting discourse and the ritual 'ruling' (Lewis 1980), and thus she challenges traditional definitions of her body and mind. For those who accept this boundary-crossing, a woman bullfighter's body and mind move into new space; they are reclass-ified. In this sense a woman's performance can be interpreted as a ritual about redefining the female body, and therefore akin to a *rite de passage*. In a non-ritual context, it is an exercise in proving that the traditionalist definitions of the female body and mind are incorrect.

There are of course many different ways in which women may experience their bodies in contemporary Andalusia, and these lifecycles of the feminine body may be organised according to a plurality of traditional or new moralities. This multiplicity of Andalusian models of how women may appropriately experience their sexuality and use their bodies during the course of their life, is concomitant with greater acceptability of non-traditional body-uses and re-evaluations of 'respectability'. Thus a woman's body will not always be considered out of place in the bullring. As I have argued the female body invested as a symbol of feminine experience may, for a proportion of the audience, legitimise women's bullfighting as a perfectly appropriate representation of a feminine life plan and use of a female body. The female bullfighting body clearly corresponds to models of the feminine body image which many of my (male and female) informants in their twenties found attractive or aspired to. However, the body remains the main battleground for debate about whether or not women can be bullfighters.

# Notes

1. An earlier version of this chapter has been published in *Body and Society* (see Pink 1996a).

2. *El Mundo Magazine,* 17 September 1995: 14.

3. By 'complete' I refer to a woman who fulfils a particular life–plan as in Broch-Due and Rudie's category of 'natural completion' as opposed to 'cultural completion' (1993: 7–8). In the traditionalist bullfighting context this refers to gender difference whereby male completion is 'cultural' (achieved through social action) and female completeness is 'natural' (achieved through biological processes) (1993: 10).

4. Thurén shows how in Valencia, Spain cultural meanings of menstruation have been redefined since the 1970s. Whereas in the past menstruation was 'shameful' it is now 'a hassle' (1994: 225). Thurén locates these changes within a wider process of change and a 'move towards a new gender system' (1994: 226).

5. *El Mundo Magazine,* 20 February 1993: 5.

6. See Kirsta 1993.

7. It is thought 'natural' for a man to be a bullfighter, but not 'normal' – very few men actually become bullfighters. It is nevertheless considered both 'natural' and 'normal' for a man to desire or to attempt to be a bullfighter. In women such aspirations are thought neither 'normal' nor 'natural'.

8. Body–uses and actions may be gendered (cf. Morgan 1993: 80–1). Although the sexed body of the bullfighter may be female, her actions may be gendered masculine and this need not be problematic.

# The Commodification of Ritual: Women Performers and Media Events[1]

The televised version of Cristina Sánchez's alternativa was broadcast from Nîmes by the Spanish television channel, TVE1. The involvement of the media with this performance was conspicuous even before the programme was broadcast. The event had been built up in the press and during Cristina's previous televised performance in Madrid. Most aficionados who had an interest in this event viewed it on television rather than live. The presence of the media was further acknowledged in the style of the televised representation. The commentator situated Cristina's triumphal performance by pointing out that she was receiving not only the 'affectionate' ovation of the audience, but also the unceasing attention of photographic and television cameras. As he pointed out, 'all types of communication media' would present these images and accounts during the days which followed.

In Chapter 2 I discussed the question of where women's bullfighting stands in relation to different anthropological interpretations of ritual. In this chapter I shall turn to the televised bullfight to explore some interdependencies, continuities and contradictions in the interface between this 'media event' and the live 'ritual' performed event. Thus I will situate the contemporary popularity of women bullfighters and their progression through 'men's' league tables in a bullfighting context that encompasses both live and media events. I shall discuss their successes in connection with their particular relationships to ritual and media representation. Elsewhere (Pink 1997d) I have argued that the meanings invested in women performers and televised bullfights should be understood in relation to patterns and styles of domestic and public consumption, here

I will develop the same theme with some different materials and in connection with the broader media context I have discussed in earlier chapters of this book.

## Televisions in the Field

During my fieldwork I spent many hours watching television in my home, in bullfighting clubs and with informants in their homes. When I returned to England some people saved video recordings of women bullfighters' televised performances for me and offered me their comments on these events. Television, video and the press provide a variety of representations of the bullfight and simultaneously form a media through which it is experienced. This media is a resource of information and experience which is accessed by both informants and researcher, albeit in different ways and with different motives. Throughout the year and most intensively in the summer, live bullfights are screened regularly on television. Live performance generates a great deal of capital and employment within the bullfighting world and in the media. This economic dimension is crucial for understanding the context in which performers succeed or fail. The live event described in the Introduction is constantly reconstructed, not only in conversation and in the press but significantly also on television. Little reference has been made to the 'media bullfight' in the existing anthropological literature, save for Douglass's (1984) rather problematic comparison between the kill and copulation that she extends to the media (see Chapter 2).[2] In Chapter 2 I situated the contemporary bullfight as a traditional event with a rather ambiguous relationship to contemporary culture. In order for their product to be a 'marketable tradition' in business terms, bullfighters, their managers, bullring companies and other parties with a vested interest in the bullfight are obliged to work in co-operation with the media and particularly with television. Below I shall focus on specific aspects of the relationship between the bullfight as a live ritual and what I call the media bullfight to suggest a further example of the interface between the contemporary bullfight and its performers on the one hand and a wider cultural (and economic) context on the other. I propose that the contemporary bullfight and the roles women assume in it may be more fully understood by an account of how it is woven into contemporary consumption and leisure practices in a market economy. A consideration of how women are incorporated into the media bullfight also offers an interesting perspective on the interface between the bullfight and contemporary media, and popular cultures.

**Figure 21:** Media attention is not solely directed at performances. Both *aficionado* and anti-bullfighting meetings (see Figure 22) become 'media events'. In this image a *Canal Sur* television cameraman prepares for a reception in the *Museo Taurino* (1992) whilst the speakers stand by a painting of the deceased bullfighter *Manolete*.

© Sarah Pink

**Figure 22:** An interview was carried out by *Antena 3* television during an anti-bullfighting demonstration in Madrid (1992).
© Sarah Pink

**Figure 23:** This flyer advertises an event to be held in a Madrid bullfighting bar. The speakers include television critics. Such events make explicit the extent to which media discourses are interwoven with aficionado social life and cultural practice.

## The Media Bullfight

Media representations are an inseparable element of contemporary bullfighting culture and an integral aspect of the processes by which that culture is produced and the bullfighting world is conceived. Specific bullfights, the identities of performers and other 'celebrities' and individuals are constructed in the various media. I shall concentrate below on the ways these issues are articulated and interpreted in televised representations.[3] The media is related in complex social, cultural, political and economic ways to the organisation of live performances and individual bullfighters' careers. In Chapter 3 I discussed the media treatments of the career of Jose Ortega Cano. Other cases indicate the economic dimension more explicitly. For instance, during my fieldwork the ex-bullfighter *El Cordobés* signed a come-back contract which bound a television company, the bullring and himself as a performer. Although he eventually pulled out (an act which in itself evolved as a media event) the performance would have been an important media event and live bullfight. Media narratives on comeback bids from ex-performers frequently develop in gossip magazines, bullfighting journals and on television. The narratives of these different representations become interwoven as new layers of the story are added – this was the case for the romance between Rocío Jurado and Jose Ortega Cano, described in Chapter 3, where clips from Ortega's televised performances were introduced in a chat show.

Television treatment of the bullfight includes 'news' style reportage programmes, and documentary series about aspects of the bullfight, however, the most dominant format is the televised bullfight. The latter has become a commercial and competitive enterprise 'concentrated on the transmission of live performances' (Carabias 1993). Some interpret this as another manifestation of the corrupt and distasteful 'business' dimension of bullfighting and identify it as a threat to the purity of art. Others, such as the journalist Carabias defend televised bullfighting by stressing the advantages it brings, such as the promotion and publicity it provides, the additional money it generates and the positive rewards of competition.

Media representations of the 'order' of the places, events and personalities of the bullfighting world offer a spatial and temporal structure by which that world can be drawn together as a cohesive whole and understood in its supposed entirety. Television and the various bullfighting publications cross-reference one another in this enterprise. Hierarchies are created in and by the media: explicitly as listings are produced showing registered performers' positions in the bullfighting league; and implicitly as importance is conferred when any performance is televised. Cordobans complained that since their feria bullfights coincided with a series of important bullfights in Madrid, Madrid not only received superior quality bulls but was allowed more media coverage. Aficionados are active interpreters of media representations of the bullfight and the role of media production within it. The connections between televised and live events and between actual performances, the merits of individual performers and the ratings tables, are re-interpreted through aficionados' subjectivities and their discourses. Being an aficionado is to some extent about being sufficiently discerning to 'understand' the information presented in the media in a particular way.

The contemporary bullfight has also developed in relation to other advances in communications technology. Satellite transmissions of South American bullfights bring distant arenas into domestic spaces. Air travel allows one access to live Latin American performances. During my fieldwork one bullfighting club arranged a bullfighting package tour holiday to Mexico; whole families booked in to see their local hero perform in the famous bullring in Mexico. During their stay a telephone link informed the local radio bullfighting programme in Córdoba. The distant and disparate elements of the 'bullfighting world are held together by the global, national and local bullfighting press, radio and television. In Córdoba feria bullfights are broadcast locally the next day on municipal television – an important forum for the public production and definition of Córdoba's particular bullfighting culture and identity.

### The Setting of the Television

Televised bullfights are viewed in a variety of locations – predominantly in bullfighting bars and clubs or in family homes. Its critics argue that the televised bullfight lacks the ambiente of the live performance, others enthuse about its informative content, some treat it as an information resource to be recorded, collected and catalogued. Viewing is not necessarily a social event, sometimes aficionados go to bars to see bullfights that are transmitted on the subscribers' channel that they do not receive at home. Others stated a range of motives for attending particular bars. For example, they might favour a certain bar in order to view with other particularly knowledgable aficionados, to eat a favourite *tapa*, to be close to home or work, or to enjoy the ambiente of the bar. Specific viewing contexts are produced in different bars, and particular social relations and resources of cultural knowledge are associated with each situation. On occasion I have watched bullfights in bars where no discussion occurred – a televised bullfight may be treated as incidental or central to the social activity of the bar.

My informants also made significant use of video-players. Since performances are frequently screened live in the afternoons during working hours they are often recorded to be viewed later. Similarly, video is used in the summer when four different bullfights may be transmitted simultaneously on different television channels. During the winter season, bullfighting clubs often screen recorded performances, usually to review, scrutinise and discuss the previous season's performances. In this context, where television is financed by advertising or subscription fees and where viewing is facilitated by either of these, or by video recording, the televised bullfight can be interpreted as occupying a 'commodity state' (cf. Appadurai 1986: 38; Morley 1995: 316). Access to it is regulated by, amongst other things, money and social relationships.

Televised bullfights become woven into sets of public and domestic relationships in both bar and family contexts. Once it has been broadcast in the domestic space of the family home a televised performance becomes shaped by, and conceptualised in terms of, family relationships, in addition to impacting on these relationships. Below I shall explore the role of television watching as 'a domestic consumer practice' (Ang 1992: 132), and I shall consider some examples of how television, and more specifically the televised bullfight, is 'domesticated into the society of family life and shaped by the complexities of family interaction' (Strathern 1992: ix). For one Cordoban student televised bullfights represented her resentment of paternal dominance and her father's monopoly of the colour television most summer afternoons when she would have preferred to watch soap operas on another channel. In contrast, for some aficionado families with a shared interest in bullfighting, watching the televised performances or bullfighting news programmes were family occasions that inspired peer-group discussions the next day. An elderly spinster who did not wish to attend live performances alone pointed out that televised performances permitted her to follow the bullfight at home.

Debates and discourses that develop in the domestic context relate to how the content of televised bullfights are interpreted in the home. Members of families and domestic groups (and those who pass through) co-operate in debating, interpreting, and defining the ideologies and issues which are represented in these programmes which they watch. Judgements of televised women bullfighters may be related to family discourses on gender roles, as may decisions concerning which bullfight to watch, which to record on video and which to switch to during the commercial break. Televised women bullfighters are viewed in a domestic context where gender roles are enacted and negotiated, rather than in the bullring where Marvin argues that masculinity is (structurally) dominant. The television is central to much of Andalusian domestic life and interaction, thus it pertains to a context where gender roles are produced, reproduced and modified. Almost every home has a television and many have videos, and this fact in combination with the recent explosion in the numbers of bullfights that are televised means that access to televised bullfights is no longer restricted to the wealthy, nor do they signify particular public occasions. In the 1960s when the alternativa of the bullfighter El Cordobés was televised the people of his natal village clustered around the television in the local bar to watch his performance (Collins and Lapierre 1968). In the 1990s such a situation is not reproduced. Whilst there are some issues of access concerned with *Canal+*, the subscribers' channel, subscription is not so costly to be unaffordable for most. Televised performances permit access to bullfighting on a daily and global scale, the media bullfight transgresses the temporal and spatial limits of the live performance, its time and location become encapsulated in media frames and are experienced in many different domestic and public domains.

## Defining the Media Bullfight

Dayan and Katz suggest that when a ritual is televised, 'An anthropological artefact, a ritual hybrid is thus born' (1987: 174). They distinguish the media event as 'altogether another experience' involving a new form of spectatorship which transposes 'the celebration into an intimate register' (1987: 194). A comparison of the 'media bullfight' and live bullfight is informative, but as I shall argue later in this chapter, it should not exclude continuities between them.

Most notably, the live bullfight has been defined as a ritual performance in which ambiente is generated between performer and audience – and it is a ritual structure and ambiente that women performers cannot reproduce. It is significant that the sensory experience of televised and live bullfights is constructed and organised in different ways. The term ambiente is often used to express this difference. Aficionado criticism of televised bullfights stresses their incompleteness with respect to this term; for example, this standpoint is represented by Matilla who writes that television can transmit colour but not art, depth, vibration, or emotion. Television directors and commentators are thus obliged 'to create a new spectacle – which will never be a complete taurine spectacle' and will attract a new type of spectating public (1993: 14). The media bullfight has been interpreted as representing 'completeness' in another way, and this is reflected in an appraisal of the *Tele Madrid* coverage of the *San Isidro* and *Feria de la Communidad* bullfights which is published in *6 Toros 6* (1992). The writer of the piece concludes that it was 'all in all a complete taurine programme which attempted to increase in type and style the number of aficionados who become involved in the bullfight by means of knowledge and participation.' The quality of the series of reviews, summaries, commentaries and interviews which were offered by these programmes was praised in particular.

In televised performances the rigid ritual structure of the live performance is replaced by the structure of the media event. Similarly, the direct presentation of the communicative body-self of the performer is *re*-presented through media communication. The televised bullfight is restructured and reframed by editors, camera operators and narrators: the event is tailored and presented as complete in a different way – both performers and performance become packaged commodities in media performances. As such they are bound up with media narratives which cross-reference television, the press and live contexts. In Chapter 2 I considered how the ritual structure and supposedly fixed ritual message of the live bullfight is threatened by women performers. These are aspects of ritual which are similarly challenged by televised representations of the bullfight.

## Media Representation vs Live Presentation

Not only does it deviate from the live performance in structure and organisation, but the televised bullfight also involves new characters and discourses. Television provides 'expert' commentary and discussion. Visually it becomes a site where technology is used explicitly to produce close-up images, replays and events in slow-motion, in addition to features such as graphic simulations and analyses of different breeds of bull. New symbols are introduced as representations of knowledge about animals and performers. For instance, bullfighters' biographies have been introduced on *Canal+* through the visual format of photo-narratives which interweave everyday lifecycle symbolism such as photographs of one's first communion with photographic symbolism of a bullfighter's lifecycle stages (such as those described on pages 105 and 114–15). The relationship between sound and image varies between televised and live bullfights. For the former, oral narrative predominates, a voice of authority intervenes in the relationship between vision and knowledge that is assumed in the live (ritual) bullfight. The relationship between the viewer and viewed is mediated by the narrator and the camera shots. The performer does not hold the viewer's exclusive attention, instead the performance is led by the disembodied voice of the commentator. Visual representation is thus controlled by the media rather than by the bullfighter. Before and between performances television interviewers seek out the bullfighters to question them on their intentions and ask them for their retrospectives on the performance. For example, during Cristina Sánchez's first performance in the prestigious Madrid bullring in 1996 the commentators speculated over how her performance was affected by her 'nervousness' at performing in such an important event. When she returned to the callejón the interviewer approached her to question her on this very theme. The actual performance and the bullfighter are fragmented by the visuals of the media bullfight: the camera zooms in to various body parts, indicating for example, if the bullfighter's feet are correctly positioned, and the expression on his/her face. Audience members and celebrities are similarly isolated and highlighted by close-up imagery. This facilitates a closeness that the viewer of a live bullfight could never achieve: the head of the bull fills the screen allowing scrutiny of the animal at a proximity impossible in a live situation.[4] Similarly, the viewer may focus on his/her heroes, a closeness and distance are simultaneously manifested as bullfighters become television stars. Contact with bullfighters is enabled by televised interviews and close-up footage, but since this communication is always mediated by the producers and journalists of television, distance is simultaneously established.

A bullfighter must dominate not only the bull but the live event itself to succeed. Once televised the bullfighter loses this central role because his/her control is ceded to the media crew. Whilst the bullfighter directs his/her live performance the programme director takes charge of the televised performance. Televised bullfighters share centre stage with commentators who define not only the performance but also the issues which are discussed. Moreover, the communicative bodies of live bullfighters are muted on television: they do not communicate directly to the television audience and receive no response from it.

In the media bullfight technology is made explicit both as the medium for transmission and as a tool for the production of cultural information, whereas in the live performance technology is subdued. However, this is not to say that this constitutes an essential difference between the two events. Rather, media representations celebrate technology whilst technologies used to produce the live bullfight are scarcely acknowledged. The technologies of repro-duction (for breeding bulls), printing, publicity and, of course, the media's involvement with bullfighting are indispensable to the live event, but they not represented in it.

## Musicians and Orchestrators

A comparison of how the relationship between sound and image varies between live and televised bullfighting indicates how communication processes differ between these events. Amongst the legitimate sounds of the live bullfight is the officially sanctioned traditional double-step music played by a brass band during per-formances, and unofficial but conventional commentaries shouted from the audience. Music is not simply a response to the visual display of the bullfighter, it comments on and compliments the visual dimension of the performance. Moreover, *musica* is said to change the sensory experience of the event by altering one's per-spective on the bullfighter – it can enable his/her performance to 'look different' and, more specifically, 'look better' (Marvin 1988: 20). Whilst musica generally signifies the audience's satisfaction with the visual element of a performance, specific reasons for calls for music are more complex and often generated at a local level. Personalised pieces are sometimes composed for local heroes and the expectation is that they will be played during their performances. A local bullfighter who gives a mediocre performance may be rewarded with musical accompaniment whereas a superior performance by a performer from a rival town is received in silence. If these motives for the call of musica are explicitly stated they tend to be voiced as

**Figure 24:** A seating area is set aside for the band
© Sarah Pink

accusations of unfairness, but aficionados indicated that they were aware that these factors were always at play.

Conventional audience participation/response also tends to refer to binary meanings implying approval or disapproval; for example, *¡Ole!* or its absence. These commentaries are not specific to the individual but they are the expression of a consensus on performance quality, which is elaborated on only occasionally. Individual shouts of direct criticism of the bullfighter's performance are usually regarded as inappropriate and those responsible are criticised for their untimely intervention. The final judgement on the bullfighter's performance is represented visually and orally, the audience shake their white handkerchiefs and chant *oreja:* demanding that the president award a trophy. The president's interventions are visual: he displays an appropriately coloured handkerchief according to the instructions that he wishes to give. It is unheard of for announcements to be made over a loudspeaker.

The relationship between image and sound is differently balanced in the televised bullfight during which audiences are free to express extensive commentaries, but are unable to participate actively in the live event. The television audience receives a detailed and continuous voice-over discussion of selected visual perspectives on the live event. The presence of spoken commentary on television and its absence in the arena indicates one of the key differences between the experience of televised and live bullfighting. The distinction between response commentaries (at the bullring) and commentaries that presume distanced judgement (at home) is parallel to the contrast between presence absence or participation distance. It is precisely because of the spectator's participatory role in the live event that he/she is not in a position to commentate on it.[5] In the experienced event there exists no voice of authority' the authority is inherent in the visual display. Nevertheless, whilst it is possible to deconstruct the media bullfight as text, voices of authority and other elements of the media bullfight become meaningful in terms of the way viewers relate them to their own standpoints. That is to say, some aficionado comments are made with reference to the bullfight, others are directed at the commentator.

## Dramatic Narrative and Dramatised Moments

In media bullfights lives of the 'performers' are packaged and presented as the life histories of 'complete' bullfighters. They are often represented with photographs and related as a prelude to the performance. Moreover, specific performances are often accompanied by voice-over narration that introduces narratives of that particular performer's career and personal histories. In this sense, rather than 'any bullfighter' representing the drama of being a man (or woman) in a particular culture through a dramatic performance, he/she is recontextualised as enacting part of his or her own life. This biographical dimension is framed by anecdotal and chronological information. Thus the performance comes to represent a personal story situated in a contemporary and historic bullfighting world rather than a general story. As it is fragmented and reconstructed in the media, the continuity of the drama of Marvin's notion of 'ritual performance' becomes obscured by slow-motion playback, commercial breaks, interviews with performers and audience celebrities and the authoritative voice of the narrator. An emphasis on close-ups of bullfighters' faces, their emotions, their feet, their technique, or their sword thrusts, constructs 'drama' in a new way by deliberately focusing upon the 'dramatic' moments of the performance. The televised bullfight tells a distinctive story; it is 'another type of spectacle' (Matilla 1993: 14).

Matilla's point represents one form of aficionado perspective on the difference between live and media events. The Spanish word he uses is *espectaculo*, a term used to refer not solely to televised bullfighting, but also to some live performances (of both men and women performers). In Spanish the term need not have negative connotations, therefore, in this instance a binary dichotomy between ritual and spectacle which criticises televised bullfights is not fixed in aficionado discourse. In anthropological terms, it is difficult to define the media bullfight as ritual, unless it is with reference to 'rituals of viewing'. The media bullfight does not satisfy Parkin's conditions for the definition of 'ritual' where 'words' are 'all important' and moreover 'inscribed in spatially arranged phases and sequences' in 'appropriate niches for verbal expression' (1992: 17–18). Whilst media bullfights can be defined as constructed according to conventional formats, I suggest that they be regarded as improvised texts which incorporate ritual narrative with media narratives. The sub-plots of the latter seize and dramatise ritual moments in media frames. It is this sense rather than as a 'ritual hybrid' (Dayan and Katz 1987: 174) that the media bullfight may be defined as a text in which media, ritual and personal agendas are interwoven.

Whilst it is useful to distinguish between media and live events to in order explore how each representation is constructed and experienced, I propose that the interdependencies and dialogue between these 'contexts' form a broader situation in which women performers are developing their careers. It is in a context characterised by this particular relationship between televised and live performances that women bullfighters are becoming successful and accepted as never before. In particular, in the media bullfight the ritual structure and production of ambiente which are problematic for women performers (or conversely which women bullfighters problematise) are less restricting.[6]

The interdependencies between the acceptance and success of women bullfighters as live performers and their success in the media are vital to an understanding of their popularity. Most of my informants based their judgements on women bullfighters on media reports and televised bullfights. During my stay in Córdoba no women bullfighters performed in the city. Nevertheless, women performers appeared regularly on television and it was through watching televised performances and actually meeting one woman performer who gave a talk in Córdoba that my informants began to commit themselves to either positive or negative evaluations of her ability and potential. This inspired one informant to travel to Malaga to see her perform, several others suggested that we should attend her next nearby performance. The media context is clearly a significant domain for a bullfighter's career-building. Simultaneously it is a context in which performers are commodified, and at certain points in their careers the fluctuations in their economic value for spectators, managers and bullring contractors become quite explicit.[7]

### Bodies on the Screen

Whilst television forms part of a situation in which women bullfighters are becoming popular, it does not offer a gender-neutral context; technological representations and practices tend to reference existing notions of, and debates about, gender. The commodification and evaluation of men and women performers likewise refers to particular ideologies, knowledge and criteria.

In Chapter 7 I have stressed how the presence of the female body in the bullring rarely passes without comment. In media narration similar themes are developed. On more than one occasion I have

heard television commentators represent this in terms of 'the body
of a woman' with the mind of a 'male' bullfighter, thereby implying
an incongruity between a woman's mind (or mentality) and the
profession of the bullfighter. Close-up imagery extends to the
audience an invitation to gaze at the construction of this hybrid
creature with a masculine mind and a female body.

In my experience and according to press and interview reports
of women's live performances some members of the audience
inevitably delight in shouting traditionalist remarks upon the
physical appearance, 'sexiness' or gender role ambiguity of women
performer, for instance, 'nice bum' and 'women belong in the
kitchen' were quite common remarks. More politely, two male
commentators of a televised novillada bullfight in Badajoz, Spain
repeatedly mentioned the attractiveness of Cristina Sánchez;
announced her before her performance as 'La guapa torera, Cristina
Sánchez . . . una bellisima mujer . . .' ('The pretty bullfighter, Cristina
Sánchez . . . a lovely woman') and later during her performance they
commented that she is '. . . guapa de verdad, guapa, guapa' ('truly
pretty . . ..'). Cristina shared this bullfight with two male novilleros,
and my interpretation was that the commentary on her performance
was voiced in much more patronising tones than those used for the
two male participants: both her performance and the commentators'
verbal interventions were thereby gendered. Whilst both the
audience's and commentators' remarks expressed traditional masculinities, they differed insofar as they intersected with variables of
class, education, and expectations of appropriate behaviour. Media
commentaries by men usually focused on Cristina's beauty and the
history of feminised bullfighting over the last one-and-a-half
centuries. These referred to discourses also represented in public
speaking, conversation, the gossip press and academic work (see
Chapter 6). The woman bullfighter's plea of 'when I am performing
see me as a professional, not as a woman' is not a simple demand
for the viewer to respond to when he/she is constantly reminded
visually and aurally that the person bullfighting is a woman.
Nevertheless, my informants expressed different responses to such
commentaries, some considered them inappropriate or 'sexist',
others were not bothered and shrugged their shoulders, saying that
such language was inevitable.

Whilst televised performances are heavily laden with many of the
assumptions which problematise women bullfighters (or that make
women bullfighters a problem for the bullfight), other perspectives

come into play both within the media text and through audience subjectivities. Moreover, technology constructs a context in which gender debate may be represented differently from the way in which it is expressed in the arena. Supportive voices can be heard quite clearly in the bullfighting media as women are making a notable entry into the bullfighting world as journalists, critics and photographers, thereby becoming the active producers of bullfighting culture (see Chapter 4). For example, the challenge made by the presence of women performers in the bullring is sometimes articulated in the form of debate in media discourses. Women bullfighters are not simply a novel curiosity on television but they also tend to provoke interesting commentaries precisely because they invoke some pertinent questions.

In Chapter 7 I discussed various ways in which the body of the female bullfighter is interpreted, and in Chapter 6 I argued that whilst the body's shape is emphasised by the tightly fitting traje de luces, this costume is not necessarily inappropriate. The particular way in which the body is looked at in both live and televised performances is also highly significant. Sometimes on television these issues are made explicit. For example, in 1994 one of Cristina Sanchez's performances was broadcast on Spanish television. The male commentator expressed his approval through a discourse on feminine beauty in terms similar to those my informant used to represent Antonita (see page 3). The commentator's description of Cristina as 'truly beautiful' was received critically by his woman co-commentator who pointed out that their task was not to discuss her beauty, but to observe her ability as a bullfighter.

Competing ideas about how one should speak of and look at women are congruent with the different discourses about gender that I discussed in Chapter 1. Similarly, the question of whether the audience should be looking at her body or assessing her toreo – is not resolved, but forms part of an ongoing debate. However, in my experience voice-over commentaries usually remained unchallenged within the media text and tended to treat men and women performers differently. Male performers are also subject to a media gaze, but men commentators speaking from a standpoint of traditional masculinity would gender themselves and the bullfighters accordingly when appraising performance and in their treatments of the body. During the 1993 bullfighting season the trousers of one male bullfighter were caught and torn by the bull's horn. He was not injured but the tear revealed his penis which, hanging outside

his clothing for the remainder of the performance, provided a promising visual opportunity. The camera zoomed in for a close-up thus
creating a curious media moment. This particular clip was screened
several times unaccompanied, as far as I know, by public comment,
complaint or debate. Whilst traditionalists insist that breasts or a
vagina are out of place in the bullring (see Chapter 7) a penis appears
to be well situated enough for its presence to remain uncontroversial.
The frequent references by male commentators to the body of a
woman with the mind of a bullfighter/man classify the woman
bullfighter as a biological or medical and scientific novelty (as did
some of my informants – see Chapter 7). The televised close-up
images of Cristina Sánchez, pulling what one informant identified
as 'masculine' facial expressions in her preparations for the kill,
could be interpreted as an affirmation that she embodies masculinity
and femininity. Whether or not the femininity/masculinity she may
be seen to embody is thought of as problematic depends on the
subjective interpretation of the viewer. Since television audiences do
not necessarily 'trust' the opinions of commentators and critics, and
it is felt that the ambiente of the bullfight is not transmitted by
television, the televised bullfight provides a complex context for the
evaluation of women bullfighters, which is remoulded in the
multiple spaces in which it is viewed.

The frequently occurring television transmission has introduced
new ways of watching the bullfight which involve various forms of
participation, a geographical 'closing' and a greater accessibility.
Cristina Sánchez has entered the bullfighting profession during
this epoch and it is under these circumstances that she has been
seen, and approved, or disapproved by a great number of bullfight
aficionados. As such she has been defined by television – by the
cameras and by the commentators. Her body, her face, her hairstyle,
her bullfighting skills, and since her father performs with her, her
'appropriate' kinship links are represented on television as well as in
other media (see Chapter 5) . Male bullfighters are subject to similar
scrutiny, however, the dynamics of the relationship between viewer
and viewed vary not only according to the sex of the bullfighter, but
in Strathern's words, 'in what kinds of bodies are the eyes of [the
viewer] set' (1993: 42).

### Successful, Safe, Novelties

Women bullfighters are often thus constructed by the media as
novelties, albeit successful novelties. I suggest that this veneer of

novelty makes them appear less threatening to the hegemonic masculinity of traditionalist bullfighting discourse: how many such rare hybrid creatures with female bodies and masculine minds are likely to exist in the 'natural' world? The use of naturalistic metaphors to suggest that women bullfighters are unnatural and unlikely to recur with any frequency helps to make them more acceptable. When defined as such they present no insurmountable challenge to the traditional order of the bullfighting world.

If women bullfighters are able to attract media attention, publicity, popularity and performance contracts through a combination of appreciation of their technical skill and recognition of their novelty value such a compromise may represent their most rapid route to recognition. I have described in Chapter 5 how Cristina Sánchez was adopted by the media when she began her career as the star pupil of the Madrid bullfighting school in a televised event. She is regularly featured in the press and her performances are approved of in terms of their technical and aesthetic value. She wins contracts and draws crowds. Television alone does not implement this process, the crowd and the contract-makers are also active agents. Nevertheless, the media plays an important role in facilitating her success, as it also does for men performers, some of whom, particularly those who are sons of celebrities, are invested with novelty value. For every bullfight that most aficionados attend they watch many more on television. Media representations of live events on television, press coverage and reportage of performers and performances help aficionados decide which performers they will spend their money on expensive tickets in order to see. The bullfight may have the characteristics of a ritual but it is also, on the one hand, a media event transmitted into the domestic space of many households and on the other a commercial enterprise driven by economic and market forces, influenced by advertising and publicity campaigns and riddled with power networks and corruption.

The key to becoming a successful performer involves no simple formula and entails contact with the expansive domains through which bullfighting is produced and reproduced. For example, whilst ambiente is central for the purist aficionados of live bullfights, being able to create ambiente is not necessarily the only prerequisite to becoming a successful and popular performer. Furthermore, ambiente is not a fixed concept but it is perceived subjectively. Indeed some informants argued that ambiente is produced at women bullfighters' performances, and on occasion consensus is apparent.

## The Bullfight Consumed

The relationship between the bullfight as ritual performance, the current popularity of women performers, and the media can be usefully understood in the wider context of consumption and commodification. New technologies, global networks and increasing access to media performances have facilitated the development of a media domain of bullfighting culture in which some of its dominant discourses are played out. Television supports women's entry into the bullfighting league tables but technology is not gender-neutral and through it current discourses and ideologies of gender tend to be reproduced. However, the fact that it presents both women performers and the issues they provoke on a wide public stage and to a diverse audience is significant.

The role of the media brings economics to the forefront of bullfighting culture in a particular way. Financial relationships between bullrings and television companies, as well as, at the other end of the spectrum, the spending power and consumption patterns of aficionados are all crucial variables. The bullfight tends to become incorporated into individual and family patterns of spending and consumption. With a video-recorder at home 'complete' media performances can be saved and watched later; they are fitted into the structure and routine of a busy life and are not only for those who have the leisure of a free afternoon to go to the bullring. Recorded performances are also collectable commodities; they can be videoed from the television and archived at home. The advertising which is so frowned on in live bullfighting is an integral element of the televised bullfight. Most media bullfights are riddled with commercial breaks. The televised bullfight therefore unfolds in a context of consumerism, the commodification of the bullfight and of individual bullfighters is both stressed and normalised by the constant intersection of commercial breaks, which create the structure of most of the television viewing in Andalusia. Some famous performances can be purchased on video – and series of bullfight videos are sold in kiosks and given away with collectable volumes. Many aficionados or bullfighting clubs have video libraries of performances and some collectors boast with great pride of their extensive collections. I discovered that even death is a marketable commodity – the video of the death of one bullfighter was a popular conversation point. In 1992 the death of a banderillero was turned into a media death. This performer was killed when the bull's horn

pierced his heart during a public performance, his death was broadcast close-up in slow motion repeatedly on the news programmes of
all the Spanish television channels on the day of and that following
his death. I saw it on television in bars, night-clubs and at home.
One family switched from channel to channel to catch it on twelve
different news programmes in one day. Thus, in many ways the
televised bullfight can be neatly and simply compartmentalised.
Although it is initially conceived as complete it can be separated
into many parts. For example, some collections are thematic. One
aficionado had video–recorded hundreds of short takes of bulls
entering the arena. Other aficionados collect along the themes of,
for example, particular performers or particular breeds of bull.

The contemporary successes of women performers in the 1990s
cannot be isolated from the media context and the practice of
televising bullfights. The anthropological ritual statement of the
performance is fragmented, reconstituted and rendered incoherent
when the live performance is converted into a media event. To some
extent this televised bullfight quashes the problematic relationship
between ritual statement and contemporary culture by forgoing
atmosphere for technique and transferring the performer's control
of the event to the programme directors. Although media representations of bullfighting are criticised the volume of complaints
against them becomes negligible when compared to the number
of their advocates. Moreover, my data suggests that television
aficionados' assessments of both performers and animals incorporate
discourses relating to media, publicity, economics, and the social
relations of television-viewing. A domain of televised bullfighting
culture in which women participate as performers, narrators and
spectators appears in a general sense to have become an integral part
of many aficionados' lifestyles. The televised bullfight represents the
increasing projection of local bullfights on to a national and global
stage. This national and global bullfight is a dynamic event, subjected to public gaze and affected by the discourses and demands of
the society upon which it depends for its audience and for the
creation of its performers. Once televised it must be designed to
compete against other media texts.

# Notes

1. A different version of this chapter is published as 'From Ritual Performance to Media Commodity: anthropological and media constructions of the Spanish bullfight and the rise of women performers' in F. Hughes-Freeland (ed.) *Ritual, Performance, Media,* London: Routledge (see Pink 1997d). Whilst both pieces develop the same themes and repeat the same argument, the chapter published in this book presents different materials and a focus that integrates discussion of the televised bullfight with a broader media context. The former (Pink 1997d) deals more specifically with the relationship between ritual and media contexts.

2. The affects of television on traditional events and the relationship between media representations and experienced events is an issue in media studies (see for example, Dayan and Katz 1987) and in the anthropology of Europe (cf. Boissevain 1992). Crain (1992: 95) shows how the Andalusian El Rocío religious pilgrimage has been transformed through three decades of mass-media attention, tourism and new social composition.

3. Other formats such as cartoons, journals, collectibles, etc. could also usefully be drawn into an analysis.

4. It is not usual for aficionados to take binoculars to the bullfight.

5. Television commentators occupy a privileged position in this respect.

6. A model of 'woman as commodity' would also suggest that women can be easily incorporated into bullfighting with the assistance of media 'packaging'.

7. Bullfighters' careers may, in certain contexts, for example, those of media, economics, be seen as moving through a 'processual model of commodification' (Appadurai 1986: 16; Kopytoff 1986). On retirement, as 'ex-commodities' they may be lauded or discarded.

# Part 4

# Conclusions

# Modern Femininities and Consuming Traditions

S ince I began this project in 1991 the idea that I should be researching women bullfighters has provoked a variety of responses. In Spain, amongst those who knew something of bull-fighting and women bullfighters, the announcement was often greeted with a statement of their own standpoint on this pheno-menon or tradition. In Britain I have become accustomed to amused looks of curious surprise which ask, 'are there really women bullfighters?' With equal frequency I have received the questioning glare of 'did *you* go to a bullfight!'. The reception of the very ideas of bullfighting and women performers takes a plurality of forms within different national and global domains. This book has explored how women performers have been debated in bullfighting culture. Finally I shall diverge from the context that has been constructed as the 'world' that framed this discussion to consider how women bullfighters are faring outside the bullfighting world. In conclusion I will touch on the political potential of women bullfighters for feminism, and the interface between the bullfight, technology, communications and information. I have already constructed three contexts in which I consider women bullfighters. They are contemporary/traditional bullfighting culture, popular culture, and media culture. I have argued that it is useful to construct these domains as areas of culture through which women bullfighters and the bullfight are made meaningful. Thus, by considering the inter-dependencies between these domains, one is able to discuss how those who participate in such areas of culture may participate in and appreciate the different conflicting and/or interweaving discourses of each domain. From one perspective this involves situating tradition in a contemporary cultural and technological context. Another approach concerns a consideration of how the position of women is changing in contemporary Andalusian culture; what the significance of women bullfighters is for different strands of feminism; and how women bullfighters can be reconciled with a morality that calls for both the liberation of women and the protection of animals. In short, the question of women bullfighters has implications for a wider discussion of the relationship between ritual performance, gender politics, media representations, the construction of self and the meaning of experience.

## Popular Traditions and Technological Innovation

The 'invention of tradition' as developed by Hobsbawm (1983) and Boissevain (1992) has become a key theme in the recent anthropology of Europe. In the case of the bullfight the cultural production of tradition is a dynamic activity that performers, rule-makers, the media and audiences all participate in together. The bullfight is not simply an annual event that the local council promotes as 'our tradition'; it is not an 'attraction' funded by local government and promoted to draw in tourists and enliven the local economy. Rather it is 'big business' and participates as such in a market economy. In this sense both its value as 'a tradition' and its capacity to be flexible according to demand appear to be significant factors in its continued popularity both as a media event and as a live performance. Whilst maintaining a purist non-technological image – man and bull face one another unassisted in the arena – the bullfight is simultaneously extremely compatible with new technologies. In May 1996 the San Isidro feria bullfights of Madrid were televised by a series of different channels. The subscribers' channel *Canal+* introduced a novel innovation: in addition to the powerful cameras situated at all key points in the arena, micro-cameras were installed in the clothing of the bullfighters to record the performance directly from the body of the performer. A new type of audience experience is thus suggested through the offering made by the development of this new media standpoint. In this respect the bullfight also becomes a battleground for media competition. In the race for audience ratings and advertising money, the performers themselves do not carry company logos. Nevertheless televised bullfights must be designed to sell the advertising slots of the commercial breaks that intercept them.

The micro-camera is related to the idea of experiencing the bullfight from the performer's point of view – of seeing what the performer sees, and of knowing as closely as possible the experience of confronting a bull. The bullfight forms links with other technological innovations in the quest to reproduce this experience. One informant told me he thought a team was working on the development of a 'virtual bullfight' in 1993. Whether or not the technology is under production, the idea is significant. For aficionados learning of the potential of virtual reality and the physical experience it simulates, the possibility of experiencing the bullfight 'virtually' was fascinating: it would involve the opportunity to experience the sensation of performing with a live bull without confronting the true danger, or incurring the enormous expense of doing so with a real bull. In addition, the potential for training would be immense. Technological innovation can thus be regarded as producing a context in which the traditional bullfight may thrive by building both new domains of experience and a new sense of nostalgia. Thus both the performance and representation of tradition may take on new characteristics in a context where the role of technology alters. The virtual bullfight will introduce a new dimension to discussions of gender and bullfighting. Appropriations of technology are rarely gender neutral and it is likely that any future appropriations will evidence continuities with existing gender inequalities. Nevertheless, the relation of women to technology must be treated as an uneven connection. I have argued that television in many ways serves to empower women performers. Likewise discourses and categories that relate women to future technologies of bullfighting culture will no doubt raise a range of fascinating new issues concerning women, tradition, technology and science.

## Personal Agendas and Feminist Politics

Any attempt to define Andalusian gender relations on the basis of research undertaken in one small part of that region is in my opinion an over-ambitious project. My intention has therefore been to offer a series of insights into the variety of ways that gender is negotiated and represented in Andalusia in the 1990s. Whilst this has implications for the understanding of gender in Spain in general, and simultaneously suggests a critique of some existing gender theory as it relates to a supposedly unified Mediterranean region, I do not make the totalising claims of those I have criticised. Instead I stress the diversity of gender relations, gender models and gendered experiences in this area and the inapplicability of universalising models of gender for Andalusia itself, let alone for the region as a whole. A most important issue for my consideration of women bullfighters is the relationship between gender and reputation. In earlier chapters I have considered in some detail the question of how a woman may develop a reputation and more specifically how her reputation is variously invested in her by different subjectivities. I suggest that 'the position of women' in Andalusia is a problematic concept since the deconstruction of the category of 'woman' allows women to occupy not one position but many different ones. This approach similarly problematises the notion of a 'changing position of women' – if *the* position of women in society is not singular then how can *it* change? Nevertheless, binary and essentialist gender dichotomies are made meaningful in a multiplicity of ways in the everyday lives of many Andalusians. Therefore it is feasible to consider how women bullfighters are made meaningful in terms of people's ideas about how society is and/or ought to be changing. Thus I pose the question: How does the presence of women bullfighters become significant in terms of a model of the changing possibilities for women in society and how is this made meaningful in terms of different ideologies and visions of a gender order? Often the achievements of one or more women on a public or media stage can lead to the generalisation that 'women can [in this case] be bullfighters'. Similarly the participation of women in bullfighting contributes to a media discourse about the roles of women in society. In previous chapters I have discussed debates about women bullfighters and how these are frequently linked to generalisations about gender and to different visions of reality. Finally, I shall relate the discussion of women bullfighters and 'change' to feminism to consider their significance as a political force, or as agents of change.

In contrast to women's sports about which there exists a thriving feminist movement and literature (see Hargreaves 1995: 26) no such culture has been produced around women bullfighters, with the exception of the works of Boada and Cebolla (1976) and Feiner (1995). Whilst Feiner's work comes closest to advancing a polemic for women in bullfighting, it is presented more as a homage to the historical contribution that women have made to bullfighting and as a plea that they be recognised. Moreover, contemporary women bullfighters have not identified themselves as part of a feminist cause. Cristina Sánchez, who is treated by the press as the main public spokesperson for women bullfighters, has explicitly disassociated herself from feminism. When asked in interview if she was a feminist she responded 'I hate *feminismo* and *machismo* (*El Pais*, 21 February 1993). Later in 1994 she qualified her participation in a women-only charity performance by stating that, 'This is not a feminist bullfight . . . rather I simply wanted to relate to this part of the public which has always put a lot of faith in me, as seems logical in this sexist world of bullfighting' *(El Pais,* 26 June 1994). Her argument is that a woman can perform as well as a man, and her goal appears to represent a personal quest to succeed as a bullfighter. Furthermore, Cristina rejects the label *torera*, and willingly applies to herself the same symbols of courage as those employed by her male colleagues. She refers to her own courage through metaphors of testicular power without problematising the iconography. It would appear that the gender contradictions are more problematic for some feminists and anthropologists than for this individual woman who has set out to prove that she can be successful in an activity which is normally only performed by men. She appears content to appropriate existing categories to meet her own ends and thus she does not actively de-gender bullfighting. Cristina appears, like those who Hargreaves labels 'sports feminists', to 'accept the values of mainstream' bullfighting, thus failing to 'relate the concept of equality to wider economic, ideological and political issues' (1995: 28). It would not be a particularly useful strategy for a woman bullfighter to negotiate a place in mainstream bullfighting by stressing the importance of feminine values. Her personal project is to 'play the system' and, by reconciling the masculine role with a feminine identity, to become successful, popular and rich. In the light of this position it would appear strategic to disassociate herself from feminism, she must take great care with her public image and maintain a favourable relation to tradition. As a feminist she would, in the eyes of many traditionalists be pitching herself against the traditional world in which she wishes to be a hero/ine.

In this situation, arguments for women's presence in bullfighting tend to be voiced in the name of 'reason', the battle is thus couched in terms of establishing that the 'truth' that women can bullfight is superior to the alternative argument that they cannot. In this debate the 'autonomy of reason, objective truth, and beneficial progress through scientific discovery' (Flax 1990: 42) is sacred. This polemic can be situated in the masculine project of the Enlightenment, and thus distanced from the departures proposed by postmodern feminists that 'deconstruct notions of reason, knowledge, or the self' (ibid.). Rather than seeking to deconstruct gender arrangements, the woman bullfighter tends to use them to her advantage in the majority of her dealings. Cristina Sánchez works within masculine networks in the bullfighting world. According to media reports, at home she depends on a division of labour by which her mother cooks, cleans and keeps house. Freed from domestic responsibilities she is able to follow a masculine role. In common with the perspectives of 'sports feminists' and 'liberal feminists', such a strategy is concerned with giving women access to 'masculinized' activities but not changing a 'gender order' (Hargreaves 1995: 27).

Nevertheless, a de-politicisation of women bullfighters does not necessarily entail that they will have no implications for feminism. As I have argued in the previous chapters, women bullfighters are appropriated by the media and other discourses and made meaningful in a range of different ways. They can become icons of change, or symbols of a historical tradition, it really depends on where and by whom they are positioned.

## Women Bullfighters Online

My first contact with women bullfighters was through a couple of magazine articles published in the United Kingdom between 1991 and 1992, and a short clip from an English daytime television programme on 'Spanish culture' which showed the rejoneadora, Maria Sara on foot preparing for (but not actually performing) the kill. In the run-up to the 1992 Seville EXPO the British media paid considerable attention to 'Spanish culture', perhaps most notably in the BBC2 *Fire in the Blood* series presented by Ian Gibson (which made no mention of women bullfighters). Nevertheless, access to information on women bullfighters was limited outside Spain. In 1996 the final stages of research for this book have been completed. From 1994 to 1996 several reports on Cristina Sánchez have been published in the British press, particularly in the *Guardian* newspaper which has links with *El Mundo* in Spain. The internationalisation of the news must also be accounted for in a consideration of the global stage that women bullfighters now play upon. Spanish 'news' is often appropriated by the British press; it is significant that images and text situate the reader rather differently in relation to both performance and performer: as one might expect, in Britain more photographic and cultural distance is established.

Two national Spanish newspapers, *El Mundo* (http://el-mundo.es) and *El Pais* (http://elpais.es) went online in 1996 and have included reports and images about the progress of Cristina Sánchez's career. Similarly, the online discussion groups, alt.culture.bullfight and soc.culture.spain have not overlooked the existence of women bullfighters. Although curiously I have not encountered an online debate over whether or not women ought to be bullfighting, rather contributors seemed to have been more concerned with sharing knowledge about precisely where Cristina Sánchez has performed and where more information about her can be found.

## Women Bullfighters, Media Consumption and Anthropology

Media women bullfighters are well situated on a national and international scale and it appears that during the late 1990s they will continue to be well represented. Nevertheless, women's everyday experience of their gender in bullfighting worlds is not necessarily so favourable. The media has apparently opened its doors wide to welcome the novel and attractive prospect of women bullfighters. However, the gatekeepers of bullfighting clubs and local power networks are not always so receptive. The media success of women performers will not 'change' the situations described to me during fieldwork where, for example, the attempts of a group of young women to start a bullfighting club are ridiculed, and girls are discouraged or obstructed from training as bullfighters. Nor will it prevent the feminisation of women's bullfighting. 'Women' remain a much debated issue in the conflicting definitions of the boundaries of a world of bullfighting.

Ritual performances, media events and media narratives are literally on sale in contemporary Spain. Bullfighting is consumed (or left on the shelf) partially because it comprises an event and a material culture with which certain ideas, moralities and experiences may be associated, for instance, leisure, fun, devotion, pleasure, elation or prestige (as well as disgust or horror). In my opinion, anthropology should be concerned not simply with these 'products' and their changing content, but also with how they are consumed by various audiences. Women's performances do not fit into 'the culture' in any singular way. The culture in which bullfighting is made a part is under constant production, and both men and women are active cultural producers. Nor do women bullfighters 'mean something' in themselves. Rather they are appropriated by a range of different standpoints and woven into different discourses in what at that particular time appears to be the most appropriate manner. The idea of a woman bullfighter is invested with a multiplicity of meanings that indicate the inapplicability of a binary model of Andalusian gender.

# Appendix: Question's of Terminology and Translation

The translation of cross-cultural concepts, linguistic terms and gender (or gendered) terminology is a complex matter for which there exists no hard and fast rules in anthropology. Questions concerning which terms anthropologists should use to denote the identity of a woman who plays a man's role in a ritual (or non-ritual) context cause dilemmas for those working in western urban contexts and non-industrial rural societies.[1]

In Chapter 6 I show how everyday uses of the terms used to refer to women who are bullfighters are inconsistent. In some contexts the use of a particular term (e.g. torera or novillero) may be especially significant. Such terminology implies not only the sex of the performer, but also the ways in which their performances are classified. Thus it also possibly expresses an opinion over whether or not women should be excluded from 'traditional' men's bullfighting. Since the Spanish terminology is never neutral I have chosen to refer to female sexed performers as 'women bullfighters' and their activity 'women's bullfighting'. Although I found the latter term less satisfactory because it could be misinterpreted as referring to a feminised bullfight, I have maintained it with the purpose of distinguishing between bullfighting when performed by men or by women. In my initial work on women performers I used the term 'female bullfighters' (see Pink 1996a). The decision to change this label is founded on the intention to stress that the diversity within the category of 'women' is similarly applicable to both women bullfighters themselves and to the ways in which they are interpreted.

However, there are also some general problems related to the label 'woman bullfighter' which are not directly related to the gender theme. The term 'bullfighter' is controversial owing to the problematic nature of the translation of the Spanish *corrida de toros* (literally 'running of the bulls') to the English 'bullfight' which 'gives an immediately false impression of its character . . . men do not fight bulls; only the bull fights' (Marvin 1988: 203). Marvin resolves this problem by substituting these inadequate English translations of bullfighting terminology for the original Spanish terms. This is particularly useful since many of these terms refer specifically to bullfighting and as such have no direct translation into English. Marvin's (1988) text thus incorporates these Spanish language concepts in a way which facilitates description and reference unhindered by inappropriate English language analogies. This strategy enables Marvin to communicate an informed Spanish aficionado perspective on the bullfight. Mitchell, in comparison, denies the aficionado interpretation of the bullfight, insisting that 'bullfighting aficionados do not truly understand bullfighting,' they 'cannot see the wood for the trees' (1991: 3). Whilst Marvin (1986) argues that in *aficionado* terms the bullfight is not an act of violence, Mitchell proposes that it is a 'national pornography' (1991: 174). For Mitchell's analysis, as the indigenous terminology would only serve to contradict his argument; he retains the English term 'bullfight'. As I have stressed, my own reasons for using 'bullfighter' and 'woman bullfighter' are very different from Mitchell's. I aim to produce a text which accounts for, but remains neutral concerning, the various implications of *torero/torera, mujer torero, señorita torera, novillero/novillera*, etc. In comparison, for Marvin's analysis, where 'female bullfighting' was interpreted as a feminised activity, the term *torera* was an suitable label for a female bullfighter.

# Note

1. For example, Signe Howell has spoken of 'female priests' who play the role of 'male priests' amongst the Leo, Malaysia (Presentation at the University of Kent, 16 July 1995). In the indigenous language however, when 'female priests' enact the roles of 'male priests' both men and women are referred to by the same priestly term which does not indicate their biological sex (as I was informed by personal communication). It is often necessary for anthropologists to use certain terminology for the purposes of describing

how gender difference is (or is not) expressed. One is often obliged to do so knowing that these terms do not represent the closest possible translation from the original language.

# Bibliography

Appadurai, A. (1986), 'Introduction: commodities and the politics of value', in A. Appadurai ed.), *The Social Life of Things: commodities in cultural perspective*, Cambridge: Cambridge University Press.

Ang, I. (1991), *Desperately Seeking the Audience*, London: Routledge.

——, (1992), 'Living-room wars: new technologies, audience measurement and the tactics of television consumption', in R. Silverstone and E. Hirsch (eds.), *Consuming Technologies: Media and Information in Domestic Spaces*, London: Routledge.

Baeza, C. (1992), *Estar Viva*, 188, 31 May–6 June 1992.

Blasco Ibañez, V. (1991), *Sangre y Arena* (revised edition), Madrid: University of Salamanca.

Boada, E. and F. Cebolla (1976), *Las Señoritas Toreras: historia, erótica y politica del toreo feminino*, Madrid: Ediciones Felmar.

Boissevain, J. (1992), 'Introduction', J. Boissevain (ed.), *Revitalizing European Rituals*, London: Routledge.

Borderías, C. (1991), 'Proyectos, Estrategías Familiares y Trayectorias Sociales Femininas', in J. Prat, V. Martinez, J. Contreras and I. Moreno (eds.), *Anthropología de los Pueblos de España*, Madrid: Taurus.

Borrell Velasco, V. (1992), 'Mujer y Vida Pública', in P. Sanchíz (ed.), *Mujer Andaluza: ¿la caída de un mito?* Seville: Muñoz Moya Montraveta editores.

Brandes, S. (1981), 'Like wounded stags: male sexual ideology in an Andalusian town', in S. Ortner and H. Whitehead (eds.), *Sexual Meanings: The Cultural Construction of Gender and Sexuality*, Cambridge: Cambridge University Press.

——, (1985), *Metaphors of Masculinity*, Philadelphia: University of Pennsylvania Press.

——, (1987), 'Reflections on Honor and Shame in the Mediterranean', in D. Gilmore (ed.), *Honor and Shame and the Unity of the*

*Mediterranean* special publication of the American Anthropological Association: no.22, 121–134.

——, (1992), 'Sex Roles and Anthropological Research in Rural Andalusia', in J. Da Pina Cabral and J. Campbell (eds.), *Europe Observed: Anthropological Fieldwork in Southern Europe,* London: Macmillan Press Ltd.

Broche-Due, V. and I. Rudie (1993), 'Carved Flesh – Cast Selves: An Introduction', in V. Broche-Due, I. Rudie and T. Bleie (eds.), *Carved Flesh Cast Selves: Gendered Symbols and Social Practices,* Oxford: Berg Publishers.

Buckley, T. and A. Gottlieb (1988), 'Introduction', in *Blood Magic: The Anthropology of Menstruation,* London: University of California Press Ltd.

Cambria, R. (1991), 'Bullfighting and the Intellectuals', in T. Mitchell, *Blood Sport: A Social History of Bullfighting,* Philadelphia: University of Pennsylvania Press.

Capderila, J. (1979), *La Corrida,* Barcelona: La Gaya Ciencia S.A.

Carabias, J. L. (1993), 'Zapping Taurino', in *Aplausos,* no. 832: 6 September.

Cardín, A. (1991), 'Ambigüedades Sexuales del Torero', in *Taurología,* Madrid: Ediciones Brindis S.A.

Cátedra, M. (ed.) (1991), *Los Españoles vistos por los antropólogos,* Madrid: Ediciones Júcar.

Cockburn, C. (1992), 'The circuit of technology: gender, identity and power', in R. Silverstone and E. Hirsch (eds.), *Consuming Technologies: Media and Information in Domestic Spaces,* London: Routledge.

Collins, L. and D. Lapierre (1968) *Or I'll dress you in mourning: the extraordinary story of El Cordobés and the new Spain he stands for,* London: Weidenfeld and Nicholson.

Connell, R. W. (1987), *Gender and Power,* Cambridge: Polity Press.

——, (1995), *Masculinities,* Cambridge: Polity Press.

Conrad, B. (1952), *Death of a Matador,* London: New English Library.

——, (1960 [1961]), 'Introduction' to L. Verill Cintrón, *Goddess of the Bullring: The Story of Conchita Cintrón the World's Greatest Matadora,* London: Frank Miller Ltd.

Conrad, J. R. (1957), *The Horn and the Sword: The History of the Bull as a Symbol of Power and Fertility,* New York: E.P. Dutton.

Corbin, J. (1978), 'Funerals, Bullfights and the "Terrors" of 1936: Some Dialectics of Death in Southern Spain' (unpublished manuscript).

Corbin, J. and M. Corbin (1984), *Compromising Relations: Kith, Kin and Class in Andalusia*, Hampshire: Gower Publishing Company.

——, (1986), *Urbane Thought: Culture and Class in an Andalusian City*, Hampshire: Gower Publishing Company.

Corbin, M. (1987), Review of D. Gilmore and G. Gwyne (eds.), 'Sex and Gender in Southern Europe: Problems and Prospects', in *Man* vol.22: 756.

Cornwall, A. and N. Lindisfarne (1994a), 'Introduction' A. Cornwall and N. Lindisfarne (eds.), *Dislocating Masculinity: Comparative Ethnographies*, London: Routledge.

——, (1994b), 'Dislocating Masculinity: Gender, Power and Anthropology', in A. Cornwall and N. Lindisfarne (eds.), *Dislocating Masculinity: Comparative Ethnographies*, London: Routledge.

Corrigan, P. (1993), 'The Clothes-Horse Rodeo: Or, How the Sociology of Clothing and Fashion Throws its (w)Reiters', in *Theory, Culture and Society*, vol.10:143–155.

Cousins, C. (1994), 'A comparison of the labour market position of women in Spain and the UK with reference to the "flexible" labour debate', in *Work, Employment and Society*, vol.8, no.1: 45–67.

——, (1995), 'Women and Social Policy in Spain: the development of a gendered welfare regime', in *Journal of European Social Policy*, vol.5, no.3.

Crain, M. (1992), 'Pilgrims, "yuppies" and media men: the transformation of an Andalusian pilgrimage', in J. Boissevain (ed.), *Revitalizing European Rituals*, London: Routledge.

Cruces, F. and A. Díaz de Rada (1992), 'Public Celebrations in a Spanish Valley', in J. Boissevain (ed.), *Revitalizing European Rituals*, London: Routledge.

Davis, F. (1992), *Fashion, Culture and Identity*, Chicago/London: University of Chicago Press.

Dayan, D. and E. Katz (1987), 'Performing Media Events', in J. Curran, A. Smith and P. Wingate (eds.), *Impacts and Influences: Essays on media power in the twentieth century*, London: Methuen.

de Aricha, A. (1966), 'Juanita Cruz, ex matadora de toros', in *El Burladero*, 6, April 1996.

de Córdoba, J.L. (1991), 'Saludo', in *Ladis 25 Años de Fotografía Taurina: Los Califas 1965–1990*, Córdoba, Spain: Publicaciones del Monte de Piedad y Caja de Ahorros de Córdoba.

de Cossío, J. M. (1943, 1943, 1947, 1961), *Los Toros*, 4 vols, Madrid: Espasa Calpe.

de la Fuente, M. (1993), '¿Si or no al torero feminino?', in *Toros y Toreros*, 38: 604–605, Spain: Grupo Editorial Babilonia.

Delamont, S. (1995), *Appetites and Identities*, London: Routledge.

Delgado Ruíz, M. (1989), 'El Toreo como Arte o cómo se Desactiva un Rito', in *Taurología*, Madrid: Ediciones Brindis S.A.

del Valle, T. (ed.) (1993), *Gendered Anthropology*, London: Routledge.

Diaz de Rada, A. and F. Cruces (1994), 'The mysteries of incarnation: some problems to do with the analytic language of practice', in K. Hastrup and P. Hervik (eds.), *Social Experience and Anthropological Knowledge*, London: Routledge.

Diaz-Cañabata, A. (1970), *Paseillo por el planeta de los toros*, Madrid: Biblioteca Basica.

Douglass, C. (1984), 'Toro muerto, vaca es: An Interpretation of the Spanish Bullfight', in *American Ethnologist*, vol.11: 242–258.

——, (1992), '"Europe", "Spain", and the Bulls', in *Journal of Mediterranean Studies*, vol.2, no.1: 67–76.

Dreissen, H. (1983), 'Male sociability and rituals of masculinity in rural Andalusia', *Anthropological Quarterly*, vol.56, no.3: 125–133.

Epstein, J. and K. Straub (1991), *Body Guards: the cultural politics of gender ambiguity*, London: Routledge.

Escalera, J. (1991), 'Casinos, peñas, Estructura Social y Poder Local', in J. Prat, V. Martinez, J. Contreras and I. Moreno (eds.), *Anthropología de los Pueblos de España*, Madrid: Taurus.

Fabian, J. (1983), *Time and the Other: How Anthropology makes its Object*, New York: Columbia University Press.

Falk, P. (1994), *The Consuming Body*, London: Sage Publications.

Featherstone, M. (1991a), 'The Body in Consumer Culture', in M. Featherstone, M. Hepworth and B. S. Turner (eds.), *The Body: Social Process and Cultural Theory*, London: Sage Publications.

——, (1991b), *Consumer Culture and Postmodernism*, London: Sage Publications.

Feiner, M. (1995), *La mujer en el mundo del toro*, Madrid: Alianza Editorial.

Fifield, W. (1960), *Matadora*, London: Cox and Wyman.

Finnegan, R. (1992), *Oral Traditions and the Verbal Arts: A Guide to Research Practices*, London: Routledge.

Flax, J. (1990), 'Postmodernism and Gender Relations in Feminist Theory', in L. J. Nicholson (ed.), *Feminism/Postmodernism*, London: Routledge.

Frank, A.W. (1991), 'For a Sociology of the Body: An Analytical Review', in M. Featherstone, M. Hepworth and B.S. Turner (eds.),

*The Body: Social Process and Cultural Theory*, London: Sage Publications.

Freidman, J. (1994), *Cultural Identity and Global Process*, London: Sage.

Freund, P.E.S. (1988), 'Bringing society into the body', in *Theory and Society*, vol.17: 39–864.

Gargilla, A. (1989), 'Paquirri: Gloria y Muerte de un Torero', in *Grandes Toreros de España*, no.1.

Gautier, T. (1975), *La Maja y el Torero*, Spain: Nostromo Editores S.A.

Gil Calvo, E. (1993), 'Mujeres. Asalto al Poder', in *El País Semanal*, no.121: 13 June 1993.

Gilmore, D. (1985), 'Introduction', in D. Gilmore (ed.), *Sex and Gender in Southern Europe: Problems and Prospects*, Special Issue no.3 of *Anthropology*, May-Dec. vol.IX, nos.1 and 2.

——, (1987a), *Agression and Community: Paradoxes of Andalusian Culture*, New Haven, Connecticut: Yale University Press.

——, (1987b), 'Introduction: The Shame of Dishonor', in D. Gilmore (ed.), *Honor and Shame and the Unity of the Mediterranean*, special publication of the American Anthropological Association, no.22: 90–103.

——, (1990), *Manhood in the Making: Cultural Concepts of Masculinity*, New Haven, Connecticut: Yale University Press.

——, (1995), 'The Scholar Minstrels of Andalusia: deep oratory, or the carnivalesque upside down', in *The Journal of the Royal Anthropological Insitute*, vol. l: 561–580.

Giovannini, M. J. (1987), 'Female Chastity Codes in the Circum-Mediterranean: Comparative Perspectives', in D. Gilmore (ed.), *Honor and Shame in the Mediterranean*, special publication of the American Anthropological Association, no.22: 61–74.

González Viñas, F. (1992), 'Porqué las mujeres no pueden ser figuras del toreo', in *Boletín de Loterías y Toros*, vol.1, no.2, Mayo.

Grosso, M. (1992), 'La Imagen Impossible', in *Pantalla y Ruedo*, Córdoba: Filmoteca de Andalusia.

Hagaman, D. (1993), 'The Joy of Victory, the Agony of Defeat: Stereotypes in Newspaper Sports Feature Photographs', in *Visual Sociology*, vol.8, Fall, no. 2: 48–66.

Hargreaves, J. (1992), 'Sex, Gender and the Body in Sport and Leisure: Has There Been a Civilizing Process?', in E. Dunning and C. Rojek (eds.), *Sport and Leisure in the Civilizing Process*, London: Macmillan.

—— (1994), *Sporting Females: critical issues in the history and sociology of women's sports*, Routledge: London.

Hart, A. (1994), 'Missing Masculinity?: Prostitutes' clients in Alicante, Spain', in A. Cornwall and N. Lindisfarne (eds.), *Dislocating Masculinity: Comparative Ethnographies*, London: Routledge.

Hobsbawm, E. (1983), 'Introduction: Inventing Traditions', in E. Hobsbawn and T. Ranger (eds.), *The Invention of Tradition*, Cambridge: Cambridge University Press.

Hooper, J. (1992), 'California Dreaming', in the *Guardian*, 7 February 1992.

Horcajada García, R. (1986), *Soñador: La Corrida según el punto de vista del toro*, Spain: Ediciones Ariel.

Howell, S. and M. Melhuus (1993), 'The study of kinship; the study of person; a study of gender?', in T. del Valle (ed.), *Gendered Anthropology*, London: Routledge.

Ingham, J. (1964), 'The Bullfighter', *American Imago*, no.21.

Instituto de la Mujer (n.d.), *Las Mujeres en España. Todos los Datos*, no.1, Serie Cuadernos Divulgativos Ministerio de Asuntos Sociales.

Insúa, A. (1971 [1926]), *La mujer, el torero y el toro*, Spain: Ediciones Favencia.

Kirsta, A. (1993), 'Gore Blimey', in the *Guardian*, November 1993.

Kopytoff, I. (1986), 'The cultural biography of things: commodification as process', in A. Appadurai (ed.), *The Social Life of Things*, Cambridge: Cambridge University Press.

Kulick, D. (1995), 'The sexual life of anthropologists: erotic subjectivity and ethnographic work', in D. Kulick and M. Willson (eds.), *Taboo: sex, identity and erotic subjectivity in anthropological fieldwork*, London: Routledge.

Ladis (1991), *25 Años de Fotografía Taurina: Los Califas (1965–1990)*, Córdoba: Publicaciones del Monte de Piedad y Caja de Ahorros de Córdoba.

Lawrence, D. (1988), 'Menstrual Politics: Women and Pigs in Rural Portugal', in T. Buckley and A. Gottleib (eds.), *Blood Magic: The Anthropology of Menstruation*, London: University of California Press Ltd.

Lever, A. (1986), 'Honour as a Red Herring', in *Critique of Anthropology*, vol.6, no.3: 83–106.

Lewis, G. (1980), *Day of Shining Red: An Essay in Understanding Ritual*, Cambridge: Cambridge University Press.

Lindisfarne, N. (1994), 'Variant Masculinities, variant virginities: rethinking "honour and shame"', in A. Cornwall and N. Lindisfarne (eds.), *Dislocating Masculinity: Comparative Ethnographies*,

London: Routledge.

Loizos, P. (1992), 'User-Friendly Ethnography?', in J. da Pina Cabral and J. Campbell (eds.), *Europe Observed: Anthropological Fieldwork in Southern Europe*, London: Macmillan.

López Pinillos, J. (1991 [1911]), *Las Aguilas*, Spain: Ediciones Turner.

Luque (1993), 'Las Chicas son guerreras', in *Diario de Córdoba*, 28 November 1993.

MacClancey, J. (1996), 'Female Bullfighting, Gender Stereotyping and the State', in J. MacClancey (ed.), *Sport, Identiy and Ethnicity*, Oxford: Berg Publishers.

Maña, J. (1993), *La Tribuna* November, Córdoba.

Mansfield, A. and B. McGinn. (1992), 'Pumping Iron: The muscular and the feminine', in S. Scott and D. Morgan (eds.), *Body Matters*, London: The Falmer Press.

Martin, E. (1987), *The Woman in the Body: A Cultural Analysis of Reproduction*, England: Open University Press.

Martin, E. (1988), 'Premenstrual Syndrome: Discipline, Work, and Anger in Late Industrial Societies', in T. Buckley and A. Gottleib (eds.), *Blood Magic: The Anthropology of Menstruation*, London: University of California Press Ltd.

Martín, F. (1981), 'Mayo Cordobés', in *Diario de Córdoba*, 3 May 1981: 15.

Marvin, G. (1986), 'Honour, Integrity and the Problem of Violence in the Spanish Bullfight', in D. Riches (ed.), *The Anthropology of Violence*, Oxford: Basil Blackwell.

——, (1988), *Bullfight*, Oxford: Basil Blackwell.

Matilla, J. L. (1993), 'Corridas de Toros por Television', in *El Ruedo*, no.87, 1 January 1993.

McElhinny, B. (1994), 'An economy of affect: objectivity, masculinity and the gendering of police work', in A. Cornwall and N. Lindisfarne (eds.), *Dislocating Masculinity: Comparative Ethnographies*, London: Routledge.

McRobbie, A. (1991), *Feminism and Youth Culture: From Jackie to Just Seventeen*, London: Macmillan Press Ltd.

Melhuus, M. (1990), 'Gender and the Problem of Hierarchy', in *Ethnos* 55:III-IV pp. 51–168.

——, (1993), '"I want to buy me a baby" some reflections on gender and change in modern society', in V. Broch-Due, I. Rudie and T. Bleie (eds.), *Carved Flesh Cast Selves: Gendered Symbols and Social Practices*, Oxford: Berg Publishers.

Mira, F. (1984), *Manolete: Vida y Tragedia*, Spain: Edita Salvador

Pascual Benet.

Mitchell, T. (1991), *Blood Sport: A Social History of Bullfighting*, Philadelphia: University of Pennsylvania Press.

——, (1994), *Flamenco Deep Song*, New Haven, Connecticut: Yale University Press

Montero, P. (1948), *Vida y Arte de Conchita Cintrón*, Seville: Editorial Católica Española.

Moore, H.L. (1993a), 'Epilogue', in V. Broch-Due, I. Rudie and T. Bleie (eds.), *Carved Flesh Cast Selves: Gendered Symbols and Social Practices*, Oxford: Berg Publishers.

——, (1993b), 'The differences within and the differences between', in T. del Valle (ed.), *Gendered Anthropology*, London: Routledge.

——,(1994), *A Passion For Difference: Essays in Anthropology and Gender*, Oxford: Polity Press.

Moorely, D. (1992), *Television, Audiences and Cultural Studies*, London: Routledge.

——, (1988 [1986]), *Family Television: Cultural Power and Domestic Leisure*, London: Routledge.

——, (1995), 'Theories of consumption in media studies', in D. Miller (ed.), *Acknowledging Consumption*, London: Routledge.

Morgan, D. (1993), 'You too can have a beautiful body like mine', in S. Scott and D. Morgan (eds.), *Body Matters*, London: The Falmer Press.

Mulvey, L. (1989), 'Visual Pleasure and Narrative Cinema', in L. Mulvey (ed.), *Visual and Other Pleasures*, Basingstoke: Macmillan.

Murphy, M. D. (1983), 'Coming of Age in Seville: The Structuring of a Riteless Passage to Manhood', in *Journal of Anthropological Research*, vol.39, no.4: 376–392.

Orgaz Romero, A. I. (1992), '"Enrollarse" y "salir": El discurso de los adolesecentes madrileños sobre las relaciones de pareja', in *Anthropología*, no.2, March 1992: 57–83.

Ortner, S. and H. Whitehead (1981), 'Introduction: Accounting for Sexual Meanings', in S. Ortner and H. Whitehead (eds.), *Sexual Meanings: The Cultural Construction of Gender and Sexuality*, Cambridge: Cambridge University Press.

Parkin, D. (1992), 'Ritual as spatial direction and bodily division', in D. de Coppet (ed.), *Understanding Ritual*, London: Routledge.

Pels, D. and A. Crébas. (1991), 'Carmen or the Invention of a New Feminine Myth', in M. Featherstone, M. Hepworth and B.S. Turner (eds.), *The Body: Social Process and Cultural Theory*, London: Sage Publications.

Perez Lugin, A. (1942), *Currito de la Cruz*, vols I and II, Santiago de la Compostela, Spain: Librería y Editorial Sucesores de 'Galí'.

Pérez Molina, R. (1991), 'Nuevos Aficionados al Toro: Imagines Juveniles de la Vida y la Muerte en el Ruedo', in *II Journadas de Anthropología de Madrid: Malestar cultural y conflicto en la sociedad Madrileña*, 4–7 October 1988: 441–454, Comunidad de Madrid.

Peristiany, J.G. (ed.) (1965), *Honour and Shame: The Values of the Mediterranean People*, London: Weidenfeld and Nicholson.

Peyré, J. (1953), *Luces y Sangre*, Barcelona: Editorial Juventud S.A.

Pink, S. (1993a), 'La mujer torera y la prensa inglesa', in *Boletín de Loterías y Toros*, no.5.

——, (1993b), 'El Toreo, el Antropología y la Realidad', in *Boletín de Loterías y Toros*, no.6.

——, (1993c), 'La Mujer en el Toreo: reflexiones sobre el éxito de una mujer novillero en la temporada de 1993', in *La Tribuna*, December 1993.

——, (1994), 'Historia, Tradición y la Mujer Torero de los años noventa', in *Boletín de Loterías y Toros*, no.7.

——, (1996a), 'Breasts in the Bullring: Female Physiology, Female Bullfighters and Competing Femininities', in *Body & Society*, vol.2, no.1: 45–64.

——, (1996b), 'Una excursion fotográfica en la vida socio-visual de la gente del mundo del toreo: investigación fotográfica como proceso antropológico', in M. García Alonso, A. Martínez Pérez, P. Pitarch Ramón, P. Ranera Sánchez, J.A. Flores Martos (eds.), *Anthropología de los sentidos: La Vista*, Madrid: Celeste.

——, (1996c), 'Leisurely anthropology and consuming anthropologists', paper presented at the *Seminario Internacional de Antropología Visual*, Taller de Antropología Visual, Universidad Complutense, Madrid.

——, (1997a), 'Photography and the World of Bullfighting: Visual Histories of Success', in *History of Photography*, vol.21, no.1.

——, (1997b), 'Topsy Turvy Bullfights and Festival Queens', in *Social Anthropology*, vol.5, no.2.

——, (1997c), 'Women Bullfighters, Unemployed Feria Queens and Women who want to fly: Gender, Identity and the Andalusian Labour market', in *Self, Agency and Society*, vol.1, no.2.

——, (1997d), 'From Ritual Performance to Media Commodity: anthropological and media constructions of the Spanish bullfight and the rise of women performers', in F. Hughes-Freeland (ed.), *Ritual, Performance, Media*, London: Routledge.

——, (1997e), 'Visualising femininities: "Women Bullfighters", "Feminine Performers" and "The Beautiful Spectator"' conflicting images or partial selves?' (unpublished paper).

——, (1997f), Review of W. Washabaugh 'Flamenco: Passion, Politics and Popular Culture', in *Self, Agency and Society* (forthcoming).

——, (1997g), *The Bullfighter's Braid*, CD multimedia publication, Derby: University of Derby.

Pink, S. and R. Sanders (1996), 'Homage to La Cordobesa', in R. Wilk and A. Cohen (eds.), *Beauty Queens on the Global Stage: Gender, Contests and Power*, New York: Routledge.

Pinney, C. (1992), 'The lexical spaces of eye-spy', in P.I. Crawford and D. Turton (eds.), *Film as Ethnography*, Manchester: Manchester University Press.

Pitt-Rivers, J. (1963 [1963]), *The People of the Sierra*, Chicago and London: University of Chicago Press.

——, (1977), *The Fate of Shechem or the Politics of Sex*, Cambridge: Cambridge University Press.

——, (1984), 'El Sacrificio del Toro', *Revista del Occidente*, no.36: 27–47.

——, (1990), 'Traje de Luces, Traje de Lunares', in *Taurología*, 2: 62–69.

——, (1993), 'The Spanish Bullfight and Kindred Activities', in *Anthropology Today*, vol.9, no.4.

——, (1995), 'Taurolatrías: la Santa Verónica y el Toro de Vega', in P. Romero de Solís (ed.), *Sacrificio y Tauromaquia en España y América*, Seville: University of Seville.

Press, I. (1979), *The City as Context: Urbanism and Behavioural Constraints in Seville*, Urbana: University of Illinois Press.

Purvis, J. (1994), 'Hidden from History', in *The Polity Reader in Gender Studies*, Oxford: Polity Press.

Rivas, N. (1990), *Toreros del Romanticismo: Anecdotario Taurino*, Madrid: El Libro Aguilar.

Rodríguez Becerra, S. (ed.), (n.d.), *Antropología Cultural de Andalucía*, Seville: Consejería de Cultura.

Romero de Solís, P. (1992), 'De la tauromachie considérée comme ensemble sacrificiel', in *Information sur les Sciences Sociales*, vol.31, no.3: 531–550, London: Sage.

——, (ed.) (1995), *Sacrificio y Tauromaquia en España y América*, Seville: University of Seville.

Saez Boil, I. (n.d), *Antología del Toreo a Caballo*, Spain: Publisher unknown.

Said, E. (1978), *Orientalism*, New York: Pantheon.

Sánchez Gonzalez, R. (1993), 'La Ciencia al Servicio del Arte', in *La Imagen de La Fiesta: Fotografía Taurina en Córdoba*, Córdoba: Artes Graficas Rodriguez, S.L.

Sanchíz, P. (ed.) (1992), *Mujer Andaluza ¿la caída de un mito?*, Seville, Spain: Muñoz Moya Montraveta editores.

Sardo, (1996), 'Marta: Rainha da tourada', in *Pública* 16 magazine supplement *Público* 2373, 8 September 1996: 56.

Scott, S. and D. Morgan (eds.) (1993), *Body Matters*, London: The Falmer Press.

Sekula, A. (1989), 'The Body and the Archive', in R. Bolton (ed.), *The Contest of Meaning: Critical Histories of Photography*, Cambridge, Massachusetts and London: M.I.T. Press.

Serran Pagan, G. (1980), 'La fábula de Alcalá y la realidad histórica de Grazelema', in *Revista Española de Investigaciones Sociológicas*.

Stolke, V. (1993), 'Is sex to gender as race is to ethnicity?', in T. del Valle (ed.), *Gendered Anthropology*, London: Routledge.

Strathern, M. (1988), *The Gender of the Gift*, Berkeley: University of California Press.

———, (1992), 'Foreword', in R. Silverstone and E. Hirsch (eds.), *Consuming Technologies: Media and Information in Domestic Spaces*, London: Routledge.

———, (1993), 'Making Incomplete', in V. Broch-Due, I. Rudie and T. Bleie (eds.), *Carved Flesh Cast Selves: Gendered Symbols and Social Practices*, Oxford: Berg Publishers.

———, (1993a), 'One-Legged Gender', in *Visual Anthropology Review*, 'Special Issue: Feminist Approaches to the Visualization of Culture', vol.9, no.1, Spring: 42–51.

Thurén, B. (1994), 'Opening doors and getting rid of shame: experiences of first menstruation inValencia, Spain', in *Women's Studies International Forum*, vol.17, nos.2-3, March–June 1994: 217–228.

Toscano, P. (1984), *¡CORDOBA! Acensión y Muerte de Paquirri*, Radio Cadena Española, Córdoba: Publica Jotocha.

Tremlett, G. (1994), 'Nights at the club help lovers slip into chastity', in *The European*, 30 September–6 October 1994: 3.

Turner, V. (1967), *The Forest of Symbols: Aspects of Ndembu Ritual*, Ithaca and London: Cornell University Press.

Uhl, S.C. (1985), 'Special Friends: the Organisation of Intersex Friendship in Escalona (Andalusia) Spain', in D. Gilmore (ed.), *Sex and Gender in Southern Europe: Problems and Prospects*, Special Issue of *Anthropology*, May–December vol.IX, nos.1 & 2: 129–152.

Vale de Almeida, M. (1996), *The hegemonic male: masculinity in a Portuguese town*, Oxford: Berghahn.

Valverde, M. (1992), *La Fiesta Nacional* (exhibition catalogue), Obra Cultural Caja Sur.

Vazquez Anton, C. (1986), 'Concepción de la Mujer: Concepción del Espacio Publico', in A. García Ballesteros (ed.), *El Uso del Espacio en la Vida Cotidiana*, Seminario Estudios de la Mujer, Universidad Autónoma, Madrid.

Verill Cintrón, L. (1960), *Goddess of the Bullring: the story of Conchita Cintrón the Worlds Greatest Matadora*, London: Frederick Muller Ltd.

Vidal, J. (1992), in *El Pais* (colour supplement issue unknown), Spain.

Villan, J. (1993), article in *El Mundo* Magazine 20–21 February 1993: 6.

Washabaugh, W. (1996), *Flamenco*, Oxford: Berg Publishers.

Wikan, U. (1984), 'Shame and Honour: A Contestable Pair', in *Man*, vol.19, no.4: 635–652.

Wilson, E. (1985), *Adorned in Dreams: Fashion and Modernity*, London: Virago Press.

Yeatman, A. (1990), 'A Feminist Theory of Social Differentiation', in L. J. Nicholson (ed.), *Feminism/Postmodernism*, London: Routledge.

Zumbiehl, F. (1987), *El Torero y su Sombra*, Espasa Calpe Colección de la Tauromaquia no. 9, Madrid: Espasa Calpe.

# Index

Note: bullfighters only are listed by their performance names, not surnames (for example, Cristina Sánchez, not Sánchez, Cristina).